Workplace Envy

Also by Bénédicte Vidaillet:

LES RAVAGES DE L'ENVIE AU TRAVAIL – Identifier et déjouer les comportements envieux

LA DECISION – Une approche pluridisciplinaire des processus de choix *(ed. with V. D'Estaintot and P. Abécassis)*

LE SENS DE L'ACTION – Karl Weick: sociopsychologie de l'organisation *(ed.)*

Workplace Envy

Bénédicte Vidaillet

palgrave
macmillan

First published 2008 by
PALGRAVE MACMILLAN

Palgrave Macmillan in the UK is an imprint of Macmillan Publishers Limited, registered in England, company number 785998, of Houndmills, Basingstoke, Hampshire RG21 6XS.

Palgrave Macmillan in the US is a division of St Martin's Press LLC, 175 Fifth Avenue, New York, NY 10010.

Palgrave Macmillan is the global academic imprint of the above companies and has companies and representatives throughout the world.

Palgrave® and Macmillan® are registered trademarks in the United States, the United Kingdom, Europe and other countries.

ISBN-13: 978-0-230-20549-9   hardback
ISBN-10: 0-230-20549-6   hardback

This book is printed on paper suitable for recycling and made from fully managed and sustained forest sources. Logging, pulping and manufacturing processes are expected to conform to the environmental regulations of the country of origin.

A catalogue record for this book is available from the British Library.

Library of Congress Cataloging-in-Publication Data

Vidaillet, Bénédicte.
  Workplace envy / Bénédicte Vidaillet.
      p. cm.
  Includes bibliographical references and index.
  ISBN 0-230-20549-6 (alk. paper)
  1. Work environment. 2. Envy. 3. Interpersonal relations. I.
  Title.

  HD7261.V53 2008
  650.1'3—dc22   2008016179

10   9   8   7   6   5   4   3   2   1
17   16   15   14   13   12   11   10   09   08

Printed and bound in Great Britain by
CPI Antony Rowe, Chippenham and Eastbourne

Contents

Case Studies

Foreword
Envious? Me? No Way!

If you've opened this book, it must be because the subject caught your eye. Workplace envy...does it, by any chance, bring back memories? Yes, actually, when I got promoted, my former colleague didn't talk to me for months because he reckoned he deserved that promotion as much as I did! And Smith's face when he heard that our team had achieved the highest turnover in the region for the third time in a row! He was livid. And when the audit was done, some in the branch said: "Of course, as we make a lot more money than they do, they're probably dying with envy and trying to make our lives difficult."

We need not look much further: as soon as someone mentions envy in the workplace, it quickly becomes clear that we have all experienced it at some time or other. And of course, we are never envious; the others are. We are not mean enough for that...though come to think of it, if we dig deep enough...You might find it difficult to recall ever being envious of a colleague and yet easily remember times when you were the target of envy. But don't worry, dear reader, it's not serious. Psychologists call this a "defense mechanism": You are only trying to protect your ego. A psychoanalyst would say: "This is normal; envy is an affect that remains partly unconscious, except when the person does serious work on him/herself, and even then, there's no guarantee!" Sociologists say that envy is taboo in every society and that, consequently, it is very difficult to recognize that we, also, can get caught in its grip. As for theologians, they tell the bloody story of Abel and Cain (Cain, motivated by ferocious envy, kills his brother Abel, whose offering God preferred to Cain's) and do not fail to emphasize that envy is a terrible sin, one that is mentioned in the Ten Commandments. So, no wonder we feel guilty at the very thought of feeling envious of a colleague!

And what do management manuals tell us about it? And human resources management manuals? Nothing. Absolutely NOTHING. Not only do they omit to mention that you, the reader, might one day feel envy in a work situation, but they do not even envisage that this emotion can emerge in any form in a professional environment. You will, however, find many pages about motivation, about how to stimulate your teams, or about staff evaluations and other topics, which indeed are interesting; but not a word is said about envy! And please don't believe that envy can foster motivation, that emulation has anything in common with envy, or that an "unjust" evaluation can cause an employee to feel envious! Remember how simplistically Maslow's writings have been used: the individual can only be driven by noble and high-minded motives. So don't come telling us about envy; it is a mean and shameful emotion. Envy is not supposed to exist in organizations, since it is never talked about and no management theory ever mentions it.

And yet, you have opened this book. You know quite well that envy is there, lurking in work teams, hidden behind the ambivalence we feel towards a colleague who has been working alongside us for years, masked by the reactions of employees who cry injustice because they have not been given as high a bonus as others have. So, let us have a closer look at it together.

Acknowledgments

I would like to thank all those who have supported me during this adventure.

Thank you, firstly, to Gregory who has never ceased to encourage me throughout this work. His intellectual presence and love are infinitely precious to me.

Thank you also to my friends and colleagues for the interest they have shown in my work; in particular Christophe Vignon, who has read my manuscript with great care, and Danielle Pailler, for her insight and kindness, and for being such a good listener.

I would like to thank Jean-Paul Kornobis for his input with regard to René Girard, and Sylvie Boudaillez, Isabelle Baldet, Franz Kaltenbeck, and Geneviève Morel (of the Lille Association for the Study of Psychoanalysis and its History) for the knowledge they have so generously shared with me.

Many people have helped this book to reach a wide readership in France and to be translated. Among them are:

- Roland Chabrier and Pierre-Eric Tixier, organizers of the «*Prix du Livre Ressources Humaines*» (Human Resources Book Award), and the members of the jury who gave this award to the French version of this book in 2007;
- Pierre Louart, Director of the Lille University Business School; Benoît Dervaux, director of the LEM research laboratory; Isam Shahrour, vice-president of the research department of Lille University; and the scientific committee of Lille University who have granted financial support for the translation of this book into English.

Christian Pinson (of the Insead) has given me invaluable advice concerning publishers and translation. I would like to thank him for his availability and willingness to share his knowledge, and, more generally for his support.

Thank you also to my brother Stéphane Vidaillet, and Gilles Gamot, whose deep knowledge of the English language has benefited me tremendously.

I cannot adequately thank Delphine Silberbauer, who has translated this book and many of my articles; the consistent attention she has paid to the meaning and rationale of the text, and her professionalism have been very precious in helping me introduce my ideas to English-speaking readers.

Thank you to all those, at Palgrave, who have helped publish this book. Special thanks to Stephen Rutt, Publishing Director at Palgrave Macmillan, who has placed great trust in me and has greatly honored me by accepting to publish my work. Thank you also to Virginia Thorp and Emily Bown for their consistent support.

Finally, I must thank all those who, unknowingly and possibly without meaning to, have given me the material to reflect on workplace envy by giving me the opportunity to observe their behavior in the organizations in which I have worked.

Introduction
Envy, the Forgotten Element in Management Theories

Let's get straight into the subject with three cases.

Case 1:[1] And it all started so well

This example takes place in a consulting firm founded by four friends. The four consultants have similar qualifications, are the same age (in their early thirties) and complement each other in their professional skills. The idea of creating this firm was initiated by two of them, Peter and John, who then asked Beatrice and Basille to join them, so as to create a bigger team and be able to undertake more missions.

During the first phase of the project, the group gets organized, its operational structure is defined, and the partners enjoy a relative state of euphoria. During their frequent meetings, they define the positioning of the firm, the legal status of the partners and their communication strategy. The mission statement is designed and the agency obtains and completes new missions, often in teams of two.

After a few months, however, tensions start to grow between the partners. In a meeting, Peter expresses the "necessity of setting up mission allocation procedures". Indeed, the missions vary in nature and each consultant has more or less specialized in certain types of missions that match his/her interests and skills. Moreover, most clients wish to continue working with the consultant or consultants they have already worked with, which is common in the consulting business, where ensuring client loyalty and maintaining personalized relationships with clients is essential. Finally, the members of the group have different availability schedules: Beatrice, for example, has taken on other projects and does not wish to undertake too many missions.

One direct consequence of this evolution is that the missions are no longer assigned in an equal fashion. The issue is discussed during a meeting but it becomes clear that it is impossible to allocate the missions on a "first come, first serve" basis, because they do not match the interests and competence of all the partners, and because the clients' request that they be provided with their own personal consultant must be fulfilled. But Peter insists that a rule of equality be put in place. The partners eventually agree that new missions should be allocated in such a way that each partner is satisfied with the fees he/she earns.

But that does not solve the problem. In the following weeks, a climate of suspicion develops: Peter regularly asks his colleagues what missions they are working on, how many days they have negotiated, at what rate, etc. John has become the prime target of Peter's discontent. Indeed, John's expertise is in much demand and he has specialized in fields in which Peter has no competence. The situation deteriorates further during another meeting: Peter accuses John of not doing what is necessary to ensure that all partners earn equivalent salaries, whereas Basille and Beatrice are satisfied with the way missions are allocated.

From then on, Peter and John stop talking to each other; Basille and Beatrice become uncomfortable witnesses to the conflict that has developed between the two founders of the firm. Soon afterwards, in view of the noxious climate that has taken hold in the group, the four consultants decide to dissolve the firm.

Case 2:[2] The "Winning Factor" program

Capital Airport is a public enterprise that has grown dramatically in the last five years. Indeed, the number of passengers has doubled over this period and airfreight has increased sharply.

In order to cope with this evolution, the management team decides to focus on the quality of client service. The objective is to prepare for competition from other airports and to provide quality services so as to ensure that the State does not privatize the enterprise. For this purpose, they decide to call upon the services of a consulting firm to help them modify the management systems.

The proposed changes have several facets, one being a training program called the "Winning Factor". This program takes place on a regular basis, over one day, and concerns the whole staff. Some employees are presented as "winners" who are heroically involved in a grand mission to achieve client service excellence and who must be applauded for their commitment. The day ends with a ceremony during which "exceptional" employees are given awards.

Another facet of the change is the creation of "client service teams" that function like quality circles. However, relations deteriorate progressively between the team members: tensions develop and conflicts emerge, and two years later the groups stop operating.

The management team starts having doubts about the impact of the overall project and has the matter audited. The audit reveals that both managers and employees have negative perceptions about the changes that have been undertaken: the "Winning Factor" program in particular is blamed and appears to be the source of much discontent among the staff as a whole.

Case 3:[3] A waste of a good initiative

In a public sector educational institution, a group of lecturers decide to organize a short-term course, out of term time, in order to raise funds for the department. They define and organize the project: they design the training course, advertise it, and recruit participants.

But the event suffers serious setbacks: the catering department refuses to provide tea and coffee to the participants, and the maintenance department decides to close the lavatories during the lessons, claiming that essential maintenance work needs to be done. Eventually, the participants are furious and unhappy about the overall service they have received, blaming the lecturers who initiated the project for these organizational problems. As a result, the institution is discredited in the eyes of the participants.

What do these cases have in common? On the surface, very little. But in all three cases human and/or financial resources were wasted, a project undertaken with enthusiasm went sour, and a lot of energy was wasted. At first sight, we are dealing with different situations: not only do the types of organization differ (a team of four people, an organization employing several hundred employees, and an educational institution) but the latter do not belong to the same sectors of activity (consulting firm, airport, education); and above all, the nature of the problems seems to be specific to each case. In the first example, it is a relational problem between two people that results in the dissolution of the firm. In the second, an initiative for change generates dissatisfaction among the employees and does not achieve the expected results. In the last example, there seems to be a problem of coordination and a lack of collaboration between several departments of one organization.

The three situations are apparently distinct, but behind this apparent heterogeneity lies a characteristic that is common to all three cases: envy is at the root of the problems observed.

Case 1: He who envies harms himself

In Case 1, the problems begin when it becomes obvious that the four consultants are given different types of mission, and in particular when John distinguishes himself from the others by being better able to obtain loyalty among his clients and to get new missions. Peter struggles to accept this difference between John and himself, a difference that brings to the fore a skill his colleague is gifted with and which he himself lacks. While the four consultants work together to define the positioning of their firm, define its communication strategy and obtain its first missions, and before each consultant's own specific skills become apparent, everything goes well. But when, through the missions they are given, the partners' distinct qualities, and in particular John's skills, become more noticeable, Peter struggles with the fact that one of the partners should distinguish himself to such a degree. This is when the concept of envy comes into play, as it helps explain Peter's behavior: he cannot bear the sight of his colleague whose success seems to accentuate his own shortcomings. He fears that John might earn more money and enjoy more recognition than he does. While the group was being formed, Peter had alikened himself to John, but the evolution of the missions given to each consultant and the clients' demands revealed a difference that became all the more visible. This is why he tried so hard to create a situation of "equality", a situation where differences remained invisible, which was impossible to achieve. He could not accept that John was his clients' preferred consultant; hence his request that the missions be reallocated in an equal fashion. In this particular case, there are several elements that are characteristic of situations in which envy is at play.

First of all, envy is, in Peter's case, accompanied by the need to constantly compare himself to his colleagues. The person who crystallizes Peter's envy is the person he is unfavorably compared with, which awakens in him a narcissistic fragility. Envy is always the consequence of a comparison, which the envious person feels is negative for himself.

Furthermore, envy, though very active in this case, cannot be acknowledged. Indeed, there is nothing glorious in admitting to feeling envious, and Peter's stand is to demand equality between the consultants in the name of the more noble principle of fairness. Another characteristic here is that envy causes Peter to become quite aggressive towards John, provoking a waste of human and organizational resources, and the eventual closing of the firm.

Envy is an emotion of attack that is likely to cause the envious person to harm the one he envies – at the same time without necessarily trying to protect himself. Indeed, Peter's behavior leads to the dissolution of the agency that provided him with regular work and income, which has negative consequences for him as well as for the others.

Case 2: When the system generates envy

In Case 2, the audit conducted to determine the reasons for the failure of the project undertaken at the airport reveals that the "Winning Factor" program played a negative role. According to the employees interviewed, the program glorifies what is accomplished by a few individuals, while ignoring the efforts of others. Some among the employees who have not received any recognition feel that the award ceremony is insulting to them in that it puts on a pedestal people whose work and achievements they feel are no more valuable than their own. Instead of stimulating all employees and making each one of them proud of what is achieved, the awards are perceived as a provocation.

The people interviewed believe that the "Winning Factor" artificially divides the staff into two categories: some individuals are distinguished as heroes whose behavior is considered ideal, while the others, who represent the majority, feel frustrated and unappreciated because their contributions are overlooked. Many employees eventually admit to feeling envious of the award winners and that this has led to divisions within the teams. Several individuals feel unmotivated. No wonder the improvement in the client service was barely noticeable!

In this case, envy has taken hold of a large part of the staff and has, here again, a severe impact on the functioning of the organization. Unlike the previous case, however, it is the management system, which, by systematizing comparison and highlighting differences between employees, valuing some rather than others, that has caused the emergence of envy.

It is clear here that envy does not just take hold of one isolated individual for whom comparison is painful and for whom someone else's success awakens a narcissistic fragility. Most of the employees who have not received an award feel envious (and even those who have been recognized call into question the new management system), because the new system compares employees to one another and artificially highlights differences that do not correspond to the reality of the work performed.

Envy is an indirect and paradoxical consequence of the new management system – paradoxical in that the new system was introduced as a means of instilling pride among the staff, and of motivating them to strive for excellence in the services they provide to clients. Whereas, in Case 1, envy is related to a characteristic of the envious person, in the second case, it is the system which, by encouraging comparison, puts in the spotlight differences that are unfavorable to some employees. In this case, envy does not result in hostile and aggressive behavior, but in the demotivation and disengagement of some employees, and in the emergence of a work environment that is unfavorable to the development of a team spirit.

Case 3: When envy becomes a group phenomenon

Envy is also at the root of the lack of collaboration of the catering and maintenance departments. Indeed, they are about to be closed down following a managerial decision to outsource these services. The academic department, for its part, is not included in this reorganization. The lecturers become the object of envy of the employees who are affected by the closing down of the catering and maintenance departments: they cannot bear seeing the academic department undertake a new project that will be of no benefit to them. Envy then leads them to sabotage the lecturers' project by refusing to provide the logistic support needed for the seminar.

This example illustrates how envy can cause someone to behave in such a way as to harm the envied, and in particular to prevent the latter from enjoying a thing, a resource or a quality that he, himself, cannot possess. The actions the envious undertake are not aimed at obtaining the resource in question, but at depriving the envied of it and of making sure that he cannot enjoy it. In so doing, the envious reduces the gap between the envied and himself, and as a result comparison becomes less unfavorable to him.

This case also shows that envy can take hold of a whole department (and even two!) and that it can affect two entities of the same organization. Envy then seems to turn into a group phenomenon from which one does not easily escape.

These three cases demonstrate that envy does exist in the workplace and that it can have serious, sometimes devastating consequences on the organizations in which it occurs. It can be experienced by one person, by several partners, or by a whole department. It sometimes causes the envious persons to become unmotivated and disengaged, but it can also lead them to behave violently towards the envied. Yet, although envy is a common phenomenon in organizations and its consequences are sometimes disastrous, it is never mentioned as a reason for the organizational dysfunctions it causes.[4]

Envy: a possible explanation for some dysfunctions

So, it is envy, and more specifically envy and envious behavior in the workplace that we are going to examine in this book. When is it likely to emerge? What are its origins? What, in some management systems, is likely to be conducive to – or, on the contrary, prevent – envy? What are the consequences of envy? Can it serve as a stimulant without leading to aggressive behavior? Are there certain times in the life of an organization that are more propitious than others to the emergence of this emotion? These are some of the questions we shall discuss in our exploration.

Let me reveal, here and now, one of the main conclusions of this study: when one examines the phenomenon of workplace envy, one eventually finds many examples of it and realizes that it is related to several other organizational phenomena. Taking envy into account provides a different perspective of many aspects of organizational life and sheds new light onto some behaviors, problems, and dysfunctions that commonly occur in enterprises. To explore envy is to look with new eyes at what happens when several people work together and, inevitably, look at, compare, and evaluate one another.

Finally, one cannot talk about envy without also talking about identity: who am I in relation to others? What am I worth? The workplace is an environment in which individuals constantly face identity issues and are hindered in their search by management systems that encourage comparison, which plays a fundamental role in triggering envy.

The dark side of life in the workplace

Why is envy, despite its omnipresence and the undeniable effects it has in organizations, so seldom mentioned as a phenomenon that affects organizations? Why has no management theory discussed it?

Firstly, envy is an emotion that reveals the dark side of individuals, a side that also and undeniably comes into play in the workplace. And this invalidates the managerial ideologies inspired by an optimistic vision of human beings as creatures capable of giving the best of themselves at work and of finding personal fulfillment in their jobs. Admittedly, the idea that less noble, degrading, and even sadistic behaviors can occur in the workplace has for the last ten years been widely discussed. Thus, the workplace has been described as a place of suffering and perversion, where harassment, be it sexual or moral, can take different forms.[5]

It must be noted, nevertheless, that although these studies have acknowledged the existence of a dark side in the workplace, they have approached it as an isolated phenomenon: harassment does, admittedly, occur in the workplace, but it concerns a few pervert–victim pairs. Harassment at work, whether it is sexual or moral, is considered a perversion, punishable by law, and its perpetrators can be clearly distinguished.

Envy: a diffuse phenomenon

Envy, on the other hand – and this is one of the main postulates of this book – is a much more diffuse phenomenon; a phenomenon that can affect anyone who is placed in a group and in a situation of comparison with others. And where better than in the workplace are these conditions met? Rare are people who work completely alone and who never find themselves in a situation of being, in some way or other, compared to people they work with, whether when applying for a promotion, a bonus, or a post, or when being congratulated or reprimanded. We are not discussing pathological envy here, but common envy, the type of envy that is likely to affect most of us, and to occur when we do not expect it: when we hear that a colleague has been promoted, that another has been congratulated for a success, that such or such a section of the department store in which we work has achieved better sales than ours, etc.

Acknowledging the existence of this type of envy implies being willing to acknowledge it in ourselves. It is easy to believe that we are not and will never be a pervert who readily harasses an employee, and consequently to recognize that perversion occurs in the workplace in specific and relatively rare circumstances. It is far more difficult to acknowledge that envy also exists in enterprises, because doing so implies that we can also be affected by it.

Envy vs. power

Unlike other phenomena, envy does not inspire ambivalence. Organizational theoreticians and management experts have studied extensively the phenomenon of power, for example. The concept of power is often used, by the actors of organizations themselves, to describe what takes place in the workplace. It is common practice, particularly in certain circles, to describe in detail political behaviors, to express one's own longing for power, or to reason in terms of power struggle. That is because power, although it can lead to conflict or reprehensible behaviors, is also the object of much admiration: it is associated with the possession of sought-after attributes, leadership skills, the ability to use networks, and prestigious social positions. Envy does not inspire such ambivalence; indeed, admitting to being envious of someone comes down to recognizing one's own feeling of inferiority, a feeling which is difficult to express in a work context where role expectations and the pressures to perform are intense.

Envy and failure

This is one of the fundamental reasons why envy is so seldom discussed in the workplace. Indeed, it is associated with failure, frustration, and with the idea that we cannot always reach our objectives whereas others can. It can be accompanied by a feeling of guilt, of inferiority, and by suffering, emotions that do not fit in with the model of the good businessman or woman.

Yet the presence of envy is a consequence of a society that values competition, emulation, the surpassing of oneself, and the display of success, particularly in enterprises. Talking about envy partly boils down to talking about the other side of the coin. Not everybody is successful, and even if we are successful once, we might very well fail or not do as well next time – and end up envying the person who did better than we did. After all, don't emulation and competition rest on psychological processes that are in part similar to those involved in envy? And yet, whereas society values emulation because it is associated with success, excellence, and a "healthy" rivalry, envy is looked down upon and kept under silence. Indeed, it is associated with failure, inferiority, difficulties in achieving what we desire, shameful comparison, and ultimately meanness. It refers to the suffering that results from living or working in a system that decides on the place of individuals, distributes resources, and praises some people and not others. When we look at envy, we look at the less-than-glorious aspects of how we function professionally.

Envy: an omnipresent emotion

For all these reasons, envy is never, or hardly ever mentioned in management books. I decided to write a book about it because I progressively became aware of its near-permanent presence and of the paradoxical effects it has in organizations. The more interested in it I became, the more I realized that looking at envy took us right into how we function in a professional context. The question of envy is related to that of human desire, of the need for recognition, of narcissism, and of comparison with others.

This book is addressed to all those – experts, researchers, consultants, people working in organizations – interested in the role of emotions in the dysfunctions that unavoidably occur in work environments, and who wish to help create healthier environments for people who work in organizations. I have three objectives here:

- To show that, in contemporary organizations, envy is an omnipresent, though taboo, emotion that hides behind symptoms that are often associated with other causes;
- To show that it can have serious and destructive consequences on organizational life, but that these effects are not systematic;
- To analyze what, in the functioning of a system, is likely to reinforce envy and turn it into a toxic emotion with long-lasting side effects.

I hope that after reading this book, the reader will be able to detect the presence of envy behind other common organizational phenomena and to develop and implement appropriate solutions.

1

The Complexity of Envy

I know what envy is. I know what it tastes and smells like; I know its size, weight, the physical sensations, emotional cost, and spiritual consequences that go with it. In my inner computer, envy is the virus. It has dug out a weakness in my character that is at once blatantly obvious and infinitely subtle. From time to time, envy produces powerful physical and emotional reactions, but sometimes it hides deep into the shadows of my psyche and determines the decisions I should make myself.

But because I am an envy addict, it wasn't enough to just want what they had. I envied them so much that it hurt me. And I felt deeply worthless. It was as if I was slowly disappearing, as if I was turning gray while they were still in color. I could not remember what my own gifts and talents were [. . .].[1]

A complex psychological process

Let us begin with the difficult task of defining envy. First of all, it is often confused with jealousy, which as we shall see later is actually clearly distinguishable from envy. More fundamentally, envy refers to a complex psychological process; it is so complex that envious people themselves are not always aware of it and are sometimes the last persons to realize that their behavior is attributable to envious motives.[2]

Envy has been described as a "passion" or a "spiritual crisis"[3] by philosophers, as a "sin"[4] or "vice"[5] by moralists, as an "emotion" by some psychologists, and "a complex of emotions"[6] by others, while psychoanalysts have put it in the category of "mental processes" or "affects".[7]

Finally, it is not uncommon to talk about "feelings of envy" or of "envious behavior". The diversity of the terms used to talk about envy is not merely indicative of an evolution in the terminology used to describe the human psyche and the more or less strong moral connotation attached to envy, but also of the great difficulty in fully understanding what envy involves and consists of.

Definition of an episode of envy

Whenever asked to describe an episode in which they experienced envy, people generally start their account with a description of the circumstances in which it took place. They then describe how they felt and their attempts to control their emotions and the resulting actions and events; and they end their account by discussing how they currently feel and whether they are still feeling envious or not.[8] What they describe therefore corresponds to an emotional experience that consists of triggering factors, emotions, and behavioral reactions to these emotions.

It therefore seems fair to say that envy is a psychological process that can be analyzed in its various stages: one can focus on what triggers envy, or on what and how the envious persons feel, on the way in which they manage their emotions, or on the behaviors it generates. Thus, in this book I shall examine the different aspects of envy in the workplace and shall use the terms "emotion(s)", "envious motives", "envious behavior", "feeling of envy", or "experience of envy" depending on what I try to highlight.

An emotion that can remain unconscious

Envy is difficult to categorize partly because, unlike fear or anger for example, which are accompanied by specific reactions and physiological symptoms that are common to most individuals, envy seems to be experienced in many different ways by individuals, and the behaviors that result from it can also take different forms.[9]

Additionally, more often than not envy and the feelings attached to it—such as hostility towards the envied person—are partly unconscious to the envious individuals themselves.[10] In such cases, their behavior may be conditioned by envy without them realizing it.

Terms related to emotions are often used in everyday life in order to explain the behavior of others. The word "envy" can be used in this way: someone can be called "envious" if other people attribute his or her behavior to envy. There might not be any link between what the person feels consciously and the fact that his or her behavior is motivated by envy.[11] Thus, the person in question might be completely blind to the fact that his or her behavior results from envy, whereas an outside observer might see it quite easily. For example, if Mr X gets promoted and Mr Y does not, the latter might very well claim that Mr X was promoted because he was obsequious to his superiors. Mr Y feels anger. Let us suppose that Mr Y's other colleagues consider not only that there has never been any obsequiousness in Mr X's behavior, but also that the latter has demonstrated his competence and professional qualities. They might then believe that Mr Y's accusations are caused by envy.[12] In some of the cases described in this book, the concept of envy will therefore be used to explain the behavior of persons who are not willing to recognize or are not aware of the fact that they feel envious. Thus, in Case 1, Peter's behavior is easier to understand if we introduce the hypothesis that he is envious of John without he himself recognizing that he is feeling envy. On the contrary, his comments show that he is truly convinced of the necessity of implementing an equitable way of allocating missions, whereas the other partners do not seem to have a problem with the way missions are allocated.

One way of better understanding envy is to examine how individuals experience it: on what aspects of the situation do they focus? How do they react to it? How do they feel? These elements contribute to the emotional experience of envy. Let us now describe some important aspects of envy; aspects we shall later on refer to when we start examining a particular type of envy: envy that occurs in professional contexts.

Self-comparison with others at the heart of envy

Envy and how we see others

The word envy is derived from the Latin word *invidere*, which means "gaze maliciously". In the word's etymology there is a clear reference to the gaze, the eyes (*videre*: to look): envy is triggered by the sight of another person who possesses something the envious does not have, something the latter wishes to either have for him/herself or deprive the envied other of. This "something", which a person possesses and the other doesn't, is meant in its broader sense a good, an achievement, a quality, or a resource. In some cases, the mere sight of happiness or good health in others can be at the origin of envy.

It must be noted now that envy always occurs in a social context: for it to develop, there must be at least two people. One always envies someone; envy is therefore directed at a person and it differs in this from emotions such as sadness or anxiety, which are likely to occur without being related to a specific object. Envy always implies an interpersonal relationship of some kind; it is linked to a person's relation to another: "Without a target, without a victim [this emotion] cannot emerge."[13] Envy is therefore more than likely to be found in environments such as firms or any other types of organization, since an organization is by definition composed of several individuals and as such constitutes a social environment.

A painful comparison

At the heart of envy is a comparison with others, a social comparison. In all definitions of envy, it is the sight of another person and comparison with the latter that generates envy. When it is unfavorable to the envious, the comparison triggers in him or her a feeling of inferiority.[14]

The importance and omnipresence of social comparison in our lives must be highlighted here.[15] Our self-esteem is to a large extent based on how we compare ourselves to others.[16] To measure our self-worth, we compare ourselves to other people. This process begins in early childhood, when we compare ourselves to a brother, sister, cousin, neighbor, or classmate, and it continues throughout life: as adults we compare ourselves to our neighbors, our colleagues, our friends, etc. To be able to think of ourselves or form an opinion of ourselves, we need this comparison with others, with who they are, what they do, and what they possess. And when this comparison makes us feel that our competence, achievements, or possessions are inferior to those of the others, our own self-esteem may suffer, which might create a potential for envy. Social comparison can also awaken envy in us by making us aware of what we are deprived of, of what we do not have.

Nevertheless, envy is not the automatic result of a difference between two people, but rather the consequence of how the "disadvantaged person" perceives and interprets this difference. It is therefore not the comparison in itself that is essential to envy, but the conclusions the envious draws from it in terms of his or her self-representation and self-worth. A study on the personality variables related to envy[17] has shown that a tendency to feel inferior to others and to experience the success of another person as a personal loss or failure rather than as a gain they might also benefit from—because they belong to the same group—predisposes people to become envious.

An *other* similar to oneself

In envy, the person who is the object of the harmful comparison is not just any person. In this social comparison we compare ourselves to people like us, our peers, those who are close to us, those with whom we are comparable. Philosophers identified this fundamental aspect long ago. In *Nicomachean Ethics* and in *Rhetoric,* Aristotle drew attention to it: envy is easily observable in pair groups. Spinoza[18] attributes this characteristic to the fact that individuals' desires are conditioned and therefore limited by their belonging to a group. More recent studies conducted by social psychologists confirm that the targets of envy are mostly people who are similar to the envious in terms of social characteristics. For envy to arise, the envious must be able to identify with the persons with whom they are comparing themselves unfavorably.[19] Identification to the envied person is fundamental here.

This characteristic is in keeping with what we said above about the relationship between envy and the feeling of inferiority. Envy is more likely to arise when the gap between others and ourselves is more easily attributed to our limitations than to external factors. A gap between ourselves and other people who are very different from us does not suggest that we are inferior, whereas a gap between our-selves and people similar to us in some characteristic aspects can more easily be interpreted as evidence of our inferiority than as the result of exterior factors. Thus, individuals do not envy people who are far richer than they are, because the gap between them cannot be interpreted as indicative of their failure and of their responsibility in it.[20] The envied person is therefore almost *alike* the envious and for the latter a difference acquires considerable salience: it magnifies their own limitations, dissatisfactions, failures, and shortcomings. It arouses in them feelings of frustration related to unfulfilled desires, uncompleted projects, or things that have not been obtained. For the envious this difference is unbearable.

Envy and identity

The reason why envy is so shattering is that it is profoundly related to our identity: to who we are, would like to be, believe we are, and what we have not succeeded in being. The social comparison that produces envy not only occurs with specific people, but also in rela-tion to specific domains. Envy is related to domains that are impor-tant to the envious person in terms of their identity.

A revealing experiment

In an experiment conducted by social psychologists,[21] a number of students were tested in a domain that was either very important to them in terms of how they defined themselves, or not at all impor-tant. More precisely, the domain in question was related to the career they had chosen, or on the contrary, had nothing to do with it. The researchers then asked the students if they would like to know the results of their tests. All the students accepted. Some received nega-tive feedback: their performance was below average, while others got positive feedback: their performance was above average. In fact, the results communicated by the research team were not the real results. The psychologists actually aimed at dividing the students into four groups:

- Those who felt they had failed in a field that was important to them in terms of their identity;
- Those who felt they had failed in a field that was not important to them in terms of their identity;

- Those who felt they had succeeded in a field that was important to them in terms of their identity;
- Those who felt they had succeeded in a field that was not important to them in terms of their identity.

All the students were then given the opportunity to interact with one other student, and were given a (manipulated) piece of information about the student in question. The latter student had done very well in a domain that was either very important or not important to them in terms of what they wanted to achieve.

The results of the experiment showed that the only participants who felt envious of this "rival" were those who had received negative feedback about their performance in a field that was central to their self-identity (the career they had chosen) and had met another student who was supposed to have excelled in the same domain.

The students in this particular group tended, much more than other students, to belittle this rival, to feel sadness and anxiety at the idea of meeting him, and did not wish to make friends with him.

The professional identity: at the heart of our identity

This study confirms that envy concerns areas that are important to the envious in terms of identity. This does not seem to be the case among young children, for whom envy is related to a wider range of aspects and less linked to how they define themselves.[22] One only needs to observe children for a short period of time to see how frequently they feel envy and to realize that envy in children can be related to virtually anything.

But in adulthood, people are more likely to feel envy in relation to areas that mean a lot to them in terms of their identity. This aspect is highly relevant to our present discussion on envy in the workplace, for a person's identity is more or less dependent on his or her professional identity. The researchers who conducted the experiment described above did not randomly select the professional world to represent an area that was important to individuals in terms of identity. Furthermore, in the professional world, the performances of all individuals are evaluated regularly, and those who are considered high-performance employees are congratulated and rewarded, but at the same time become potential rivals to others. It is not surprising therefore that envy is a common phenomenon in the workplace!

Envy, desire, and frustration

One of the pillars of envy is therefore comparison. The second pillar is related to desire: envy implies a strong desire to have something that others possess and that we do not. The envious desires what the other has, what the other or the system deems desirable. When people are asked to recall a time when they felt "strong envy" and to indicate to what degree their experience was characterized by a long list of attributes, they report that coveting of another party (that is, longing and wishing for) was highly characteristic of their experience of envy.[23]

Contact with others stimulates our desire for more. The fact that the etymology of the word envy refers to the gaze is also of importance here. The sight of the *other*, the objectives he pursues and what he wishes to acquire, stimulate us into wanting for ourselves these achievements and possessions. People develop partly through imitation, and what other human beings value and desire dictates to them what they should value and desire themselves (this is a fundamental postulate of the theory of mimetic desire developed by the anthropologist René Girard, a theory we shall discuss in Chapter 3).

Of course, we do not always manage to obtain what we desire, and this can generate frustration. In the study described above,[24] the people asked about the characteristics they associate with an episode of envy also report to feeling disappointed when they do not manage to obtain something they wanted: they feel frustrated. Frustration appears to be a general characteristic of envy, one that contributes to its painful nature.[25] "The experience of envy would be quite different if it simply involved noticing a desired attribute and then going about obtaining it without delay [. . .]. The experience would also be quite different if it involved noticing a desirable attribute so beyond one's reach that obtaining it was inconceivable. [. . .] [Envy] is frustrated desire made more frustrating by the imagined possibility of its possession."[26]

Frustration can cause the envious to wish harm on the person he envies. If the other succeeds where we have failed, if he obtains something that points to our own failures and shortcomings, we might very well, as a result of this unbearable frustration, wish that the other could not enjoy what is denied to us.

A violent and painful emotion

The venom of envy

How has envy been represented? In the iconography of envy, it is often symbolized as a woman with snakes slithering round her neck or out of her head and kissing her mouth.[27] In a manuscript dating from the early Renaissance, envy is represented as a woman eating her own heart.[28] Envy is a poison that turns against the envious in a self-destructive manner. The relevance of this representation is confirmed by research studies in psychology and psychoanalysis.[29]

Indeed, these studies describe envy as a very strong and extremely negative emotion, which, at first, has a "shattering" impact on the envious. It emerges violently, often unexpectedly, and invades his psyche. Thus, the process the envious is suddenly taken through can quite appropriately be called the "bite of envy". Envy is experienced as a shock, even when the envious is incapable of identifying envy as the cause of this shock. This bite corresponds to the moment when the poison is introduced. But this poison must also reach the envied person: venomous words and slander are emitted by the envious and can be accompanied by violent and aggressive behaviors. Envy can bring about the destruction of the envied person, of what he or she possesses that the envious does not. And in this regard the fact that the envious person might not be conscious of being envious is not important. In some cases, it is precisely because individuals are unaware of being envious and cannot therefore express how they feel that envy causes them to become violent.[30]

Envy is self-destructive

Thus, envy is associated with painful and negative affects and aggressive behavior. But the envied person is not the only victim: once instilled, the poison acts insidiously, creeping into the envious person's body and psyche, distorting their relationship with the world, and eventually turning against the envious. Then begins a slow and diffuse poisoning process. The slow inner destruction of the envious is revealed by psychosomatic symptoms that are often associated with the representation of envy: the envious becomes thin, pale, "white as a sheet," or green; he or she has shiny, feverish, and bulging eyes. Baudelaire offers a striking description of an envious person: "[. . .] a new pallor now relentlessly came upon his usual pallor, like snow on top of snow. His lips pressed tighter and tighter together, and his eyes were lit by an inner fire like that of jealousy or rancor, even as he ostentatiously applauded the talents of his old friend [. . .]."[31]

A popular story illustrates how envy can cause self-destruction and bring violence against the envied person. One day, a Genie stands before a man and says: "My dear friend, I know your life has been filled with suffering, struggle and pain. But today, your torments have come to an end. I have chosen to relieve you of your hardships: Make a wish and I shall grant it to you. I shall give you anything you desire. Ask me for mountains of gold and I shall give them to you, a palace of jewels and it shall be yours; ask me for radiant health and you shall never be sick again, for the most beautiful women and they will crowd at your feet. Think about it my dear friend and tell me what you want me to do for you." The man ponders, hesitates, and as he is about to come to a decision, the Genie adds: "There is just one thing you should know, though it does not concern you: Whatever I grant you I will give twice as much to your neighbor." So the man replies: "Take one of my eyes!"

Psychoanalysts, in particular, have emphasized how self-destructive envy can be.[32] Envious individuals do not try to preserve themselves; they are incapable of it. For example, in Case 1, Peter's behavior results in the dissolution of the very organization he helped to create and benefited from. But his envy is so strong that it takes over his psyche, spoils his relationship not only with John but also with the other members of the group, and it obliterates everything in its wake. In other cases, self-destruction can occur in the form of self-withdrawal, and envy can be accompanied by depression.

Thus, in work contexts, envy can hide behind seemingly different behaviors. In some cases, a person or a group of people behave aggressively. Their behavior not only has deleterious effects on the organization as a whole, but also puts them at risk. In other cases, a feeling of depression and demotivation can affect an entire firm or departments within a firm. Finally, and to make things even more complicated, the different manifestations of envy can, in some organizational contexts, combine in a subtle but destructive manner.

Envy and negative feelings

Envy is accompanied by negative feelings in the envious person.[33]

As mentioned above, envy is experienced as an intense desire accompanied by a feeling of frustration: the envious person covets what the other possesses and is intensely frustrated not only because he or she is deprived of something, but also because the other does not suffer this deprivation.

When an individual becomes envious, he or she is very likely to become aware of their own limitations in relation to the person or persons they envy. This feeling of inferiority can be accompanied by sadness—at the thought of their own deficiencies—and by anxiety related to the feeling of destabilization they experience: they might harbor feelings of doubt about their own future. Envious individuals may feel crushed, defeated, and devoid of substance.

Envy is often associated with resentment, which can emerge in two different forms. In the first instance, resentment may be directed at the envied person and might even turn into hatred. Envy can also be accompanied by anger when the envious person believes that the gap between the other and themselves results from an injustice that benefits the envied person, or from the envied person having manipulated the rules to his or her own advantage (naturally, if the other has really benefited from an unfair advantage, it is not envy that emerges, but a feeling of anger caused by a true injustice). In the second instance, the envious person feels resentful towards life in general, the system, the conditions that benefit some and not others. This general resentment is then accompanied by anger and bitterness towards life and fate, in which possessions, talents, and qualities are unequally distributed.

Envy often comes with a feeling of admiration for the envied person. However, this aspect has been brought to light mostly thanks to psychoanalytic research, as envious individuals seldom manage to express this feeling.

Lastly, shame and guilt are regularly associated with envy. Indeed, envy is an emotion that one does not talk about. Firstly, it can remain unconscious or be repressed by the envious, who might not be able to see that the aggressiveness he or she is displaying and the anger or sadness he or she is experiencing might be caused by envy. Secondly, even if they recognize their feelings as envy, the envious person knows that this emotion is taboo and condemned as a serious sin. Jealousy some-times qualifies as mitigating circumstances in a crime of passion for example, but the sanction is much more severe if it is found that the perpetrator of an attack was motivated by envy. It is no wonder, there-fore, that an envious person can feel ashamed and guilty.

These emotions are not all experienced systematically or at the same time by one person. For example, some individuals feel hatred and anger towards the person they envy, as well as guilt and an intense longing for what the latter possesses. Others feel a more gen-eral resentment, accompanied by a strong feeling of inferiority and admiration for the person they envy. For others still, sadness follows anger and frustration.

Envy must not be mistaken for jealousy

Now that we have drawn the broad outlines of envy, it should be eas-ier to discuss the differences between envy and jealousy. The term "jealousy" is often used in common language to describe envy, but the inverse is not true. This is certainly indicative of how taboo a sub-ject envy is. Yet both concepts refer to different phenomena.[34]

First of all, jealousy is triggered by the threat of separation from a particular relationship. The loss (or the threat of loss) is real. In jeal-ousy therefore there is a loss of what one had, whereas in envy, it is the state of not having that is unbearable. La Rochefoucauld[35] very appropriately wrote: "Jealousy is in a manner just and reasonable, as it tends to preserve a good which belongs, or which we believe belongs to us; on the other hand envy is a fury which cannot endure the happiness of others."

Secondly, jealousy involves two rivals who are aware of being rivals, whereas it is the mere presence of an *other* and of what he or she pos-sesses that triggers envy in us without the envied person realizing it.

A third difference is related to social comparison: jealousy does not involve social comparison, whereas the latter is fundamental in envy.

Finally, jealousy is accompanied by a feeling of loss, betrayal, sus-picion, and mistrust, whereas envy is associated with malevolence, covetousness, and a feeling of inferiority.

Admittedly, jealousy and envy can be two symptoms of one same emotional episode. Thus, the loss of a relationship and the resulting jealousy can cause people to compare themselves to their rival and to envy the latter. Or envy might cause the envious to see the person he envies as a potential rival who will take the person he loves away from him, in which case envy will trigger jealousy.

Sadness and anger are associated with both jealousy and envy. Envy is nonetheless different from jealousy, and it is envy and not jealousy in the workplace that we shall explore here.

The paradoxes of envy

It would not be fair to present only the dark side of envy. Is it always so destructive? Does it always lead to violence against the envied person and the envious himself? The answer is no! In the perspective outlined above, it is indeed associated with destructive consequences. But envy can also be recognized as a human characteristic that is likely to act as a driving force that stimulates man to move forward and improve.

Most of the time, when we think of envy, we tend to focus on the first meaning of the word without relating it to other forms of behavior—such as emulation—which, unlike envy, are thought of positively. And yet, are there not strong similarities between these phenomena?

We now see more clearly the complexity of envy mentioned at the beginning of this chapter. Envy is indeed a psychological process that consists of:

- Triggering factors related to some vulnerability in the person;
- A wide range of negative and painful emotions;
- A variety of behaviors ranging from self-destruction to aggressiveness towards the envied person, via emulation and a struggle for personal improvement in some cases.

Card 1   Am I envious at work?

Consider the following statements:

- I often find it unfair that some people have obtained something and not me.
- I often compare myself to people who work with me.
- My job is an important part of my life.
- I regularly feel dissatisfied with what I get from my company, particularly compared to some of my colleagues.
- My manager does not treat all the members of the team in the same way.
- I often have the feeling that I'm not up to the job when I compare myself to others.
- When I see someone who is successful in his field, I tell myself I'd like to be like him.
- I think that successful people are often dishonest.
- I often regret not having done what I would have liked to do.
- It is important to me to always know what my colleagues are up to, whether they are experiencing success or failure.
- We do not all have the same gifts when we start our career. Some of us have an advantage from the start.
- In my career, I have always needed to use a few people as points of reference.
- I sometimes have the impression that some of my colleagues try to crush me with their arrogance.
- I sometimes feel sad or dissatisfied when I think of my career.
- I occasionally feel a degree of satisfaction when I hear that some of my colleagues have failed.
- I tend to talk about the difficulties or problems some of my colleagues experience.
- I like to listen to the gossip in my department.
- I sometimes feel despondent when I see the success of others.
- I am never happy with what I have achieved. I could have done better.
- I have, on a few occasions, tried to jeopardize a project undertaken by a colleague.
- When someone I know successfully completes a project, I sometimes feel resentful towards him.

The more affirmative answers you have to these questions, the more likely you are to suffer from envy. But beware: if you have given fewer than five affirmative answers, you might very well be repressing this emotion. And in order to get rid of envy, one has to be able to identify it.

2
The Effects of Envy on the Organization

In organizations, envy is seldom talked about. And yet, it doesn't take long for anyone who undertakes to study envy to see its symptoms.

Incidentally, it was while I was working with organizations, particularly on reorganization projects, that I noticed the recurrence of certain phenomena conventional management approaches could not explain and which, I suspected, might be caused by envy. Thus, regardless of the type of organization, when a department is restructured it is not uncommon for its members to become aggressive towards the members of departments that are not affected by the change, or for individuals to compare themselves to employees who have obtained a better post than they have.

In a retail company, the modes of management and innovation practices of which I was studying, I found that the behaviors of the different departments with one another ran counter to collaboration, despite the management's directives in terms of cooperation. Thus, the members of one department would often find that their storeroom had been messed up or that goods belonging to other departments were blocking access to it. When goods were placed in the wrong aisles by clients, the staff made little effort to return the goods to the correct one. The sales people often failed to inform clients about products sold in other departments. This behavior was mostly directed at the department that achieved the highest sales figures and which the management often took as an example of good performance! We are not talking about real sabotage here, but about aggressive behaviors that can endanger the functioning of an organization as a whole.

It is the negative consequences of this type of behavior that reveal envy. Indeed, envy can have a strong, sometimes violent, influence on teams, work relationships, and organizational systems. Paradoxically, it can also in some cases be a source of change and improvement.

Envy destroys ties

The most common consequence of envy, and probably the most dangerous for organizations, is the destruction of ties. It is this aspect that we observed in Case 1 in the example of John and Peter, two friends who co-founded a consulting agency. When envy developed in their relationship, its main effect was to destroy their friendship; it resulted in mistrust, and in the fear that one had more than the other. The feeling of inferiority triggered by envy and Peter's resentment towards John make it impossible for Peter to maintain a healthy relationship with his friend.

Envious individuals feel uneasy in the presence of the envied; a presence that reminds them of their own deficiencies and limitations. They dread interaction with the envied;[1] dialogue or collaboration are made difficult by what has developed in the background of their relationship.

Case 4: **Rejected applications for promotion**[2]
In the Hong Kong branches of an international bank, every two years all tellers who have worked for at least two years in the bank are considered for promotion to teller supervisor. Their application is examined by a committee that takes into account the written and oral testimony of the immediate supervisor, previous performance ratings provided by him or her, some objective performance data (e.g. cash drawer underages and overages, attendance), and input from the other managers. In each team (43 in total), five to eight tellers are eligible. The total number of posts is limited.

How do the employees who have not been promoted react? Some feel envious of those in their team who have been promoted, and in some cases find the person they envy far less friendly than they did before the decision concerning the promotions was announced.

This case shows that the development of envy makes interpersonal relationships more difficult because it leads to an emotional distantiation of the envious person from the individual or individuals they envy.

No ties, no organization

This aspect of envy is worrying, for interpersonal ties are at the very foundations of organizations; they are what enables the organization to evolve.[3] A well-defined structure, the implementation of procedures, management systems, and having a person for each post are not what creates an organization. An organization's very existence is dependent on the ties and relationships that develop between its members, and the quality of the latter: "The doing of work, in turn is not as much involved with the performance of tasks as it is with interacting, transacting, and synchronizing with others."[4]

It is through their interactions that people can make sense of what happens to them, interpret events, and become collectively involved in certain actions. In this regard, Karl Weick and Karlene Roberts write that: "The ways people connect their activities make conduct mindful. Mindless actions ignore interrelating or accomplish it haphazardly and with indifference."[5] The more people strive to develop and maintain mutual relationships, the more collective intelligence develops. This capacity is all the more essential as an organization occasionally faces unexpected situations, which can only be solved if its members have the ability to understand what is happening and to create new forms of action.

An organization is neither a stable nor homogenous entity. It is more relevant and realistic to describe it as a cycle of processes of ongoing reconstruction and deconstruction of ties. And it is because it is made of ties that it is fragile, that it can disappear, but also transform itself, evolve, and adapt. Thus, the presence of envy in a team, department, or even firm is extremely worrying because it primarily attacks those interpersonal ties. It weakens interaction capacities and their quality.

Poor group cohesion

In a longitudinal study of 129 student teams designed to function as work teams in business settings over a four-month period,[6] it was found that higher levels of envy in teams decreased group-level cohesiveness and potency (a form of team efficacy), which could in turn lower group performance and increase team-member absenteeism.

Envy was also associated with effort reduction in group tasks, increased social loafing, and withdrawal behaviors. This aspect is clearly apparent in the "Winning Factor" case described in the previous chapter. In this example, the airport's management team introduces a new management system so as to improve client service quality, by encouraging the staff to strive for excellence and by commending the employees who distinguish themselves through their performance in this field. But by artificially distinguishing some employees as "heroes", this program causes many employees to become envious. Whereas performance and success used to be seen as the result of teamwork and collective effort, they are now considered as individual achievements. The resulting envy is accompanied by demotivation of the staff and destruction of the ties that are essential to the realization of the overall objective. Consequently, teamwork, which is essential to improving client service quality, is hampered.

Destruction of the ties can also occur at a more general level. For example, in the educational institution case I described earlier, the catering and maintenance staff decide not to cooperate with the lecturers because the management's decision to outsource certain activities does not concern the education department. Feeling envious, the two departments in question dissociate themselves from the educational staff and, as a consequence, the service provided by the latter – and therefore the institution as a whole – failed to meet the participants' expectations. Under the influence of envy, the ties between the departments dissolve and the organization can no longer function correctly.

Thus, the main effect of envy is to damage the relations and ties that exist within organizations, either between individuals or between departments and groups. Envy prevents cohesion; it damages, dismantles, and destroys the very foundations of the organization.[7]

Dissatisfaction with work and withdrawal

Envious people often have negative feelings towards:

- themselves since envy is related to a feeling of inferiority;
- the person they envy, whom they can resent, be angry with, or even hate;
- the system, considered frustrating and unfair.

It is hardly surprising therefore that envy in the workplace is accompanied by a dissatisfaction with work. This dissatisfaction can take a number of forms.

A study involving 222 individuals with managerial jobs in the industrial and service sectors[8] shows a clear link between dissatisfaction with work and the feeling of envy. When individuals are envious of colleagues – whom, they feel, benefit from more support and are better appreciated than they are – they also feel less satisfied with work than the individuals who are not (or less) envious. This is hardly surprising since, when they compare themselves to others, the envious feel that they are worth less than the others and consequently can only see what is unsatisfactory and disappointing in their own situation. Envy is associated with frustration and bitterness. It throws a gray cover over everything. To envious individuals everything is dull; they feel that their situation is nowhere near what they desire or what they believe is desirable from the point of view of people who are better off than they are. By a contrast effect, envy then enhances the projects that have failed; the desires and wishes the envious individuals have not fulfilled. Envy is always associated with a gap between a real situation and an ideal, or at least better, situation. So no wonder it is accompanied with a feeling of dissatisfaction!

Moreover, as envy decreases group cohesiveness and potency, it also diminishes group satisfaction. The above-mentioned study of 129 student teams shows this relation quite clearly.

A bad relationship with one's manager

Envious people also tend to feel unhappy about their relationships with their direct superiors,[9] whereas when people feel that they are appreciated by their managers, that they are treated equitably and fairly, the feeling of envy tends to subside.[10] In general, different employees have different types of relationships with their managers. Some feel that their relationship with their superior is based on trust and respect, that their manager understands them, and that they have formed a good relationship. Others establish a distant and formal relationship based on their compliance to certain rules, rather than a personal and therefore more emotionally involved relationship. People who enjoy good relationships with their boss tend to stay in their team for longer, are more satisfied with their job, and find their work more fulfilling.[11] In the above-mentioned survey of

222 managers, the individuals who feel envious also feel that their relationship with their direct superior is poor. It is difficult to determine which is the cause and which is the effect (the study gives no explanation in this regard): does feeling envious lead to resentment against the system as a whole or more specifically towards the direct superiors, who are the representatives of this system? Or is it because employees do not get on with their boss that they tend to think that the latter favors some team members over others and therefore contributes to the development of envy? Whatever the answer might be, the fact that envy comes with a perceived poor relationship between employees and their boss does nothing to make the envious individuals feel more satisfied at work.

Self-isolation and depression

As discussed in Chapter 1, one of the central aspects of envy is the fact that envious individuals tend to compare themselves unfavorably to others, and as a result feel inferior to others. The consequent risk is that they might not be able to overcome this feeling of inferiority and might get stuck in the belief that the gap between the others and themselves is related to their own shortcomings. The psychiatrist Harry Stack Sullivan[12] phrased this point:

> Envy is not pleasant because any formulation of it – any implicit process connected with it – necessarily starts with the point that you need something, some material thing that, unhappily, someone else has. This easily leads to the question, "Why don't you have it?" And that is itself enough in some cases to provoke insecurity, for apparently the other fellow is better at assembling these material props of security than you are, which makes you even more inferior.

Envy can lead to depressive behavior.[13] The depressive aspect of envy is caused by the difficulty the envious have in freeing themselves from an annihilating feeling of inferiority that undermines their self-image. The envious can then be incapable of restoring the cognitive and emotional balance they need to be able to undertake new projects. Why should they try and move forward when everything they undertake ends up pointing to their limitations and their inability to succeed? Why persist in wishing for something they are incapable of achieving, but which other people do achieve? Envy can degenerate into depression when the answers to these types of question generate a lasting feeling of impotence and cause them to close in on themselves. The envious might also avoid competition and occasions of comparison as the latter leave them in excruciating doubt about their own abilities.[14]

One of the cases of workplace envy I studied provides a good illustration of how envy can lead to self-withdrawal and to a paralyzing fear of failure, of not being up to the job, when the other is successful and appears to possess what seems inaccessible to the envious.[15]

Case 5: **Fanny and Cecilia**

Fanny and Cecilia are two students from the same year. They are both performing on-the-job training at the purchase center of a large distribution group. Both work in the "outdoor leisure" section, one in the gardening department, and the other in the sports department. The two students are "almost alike": they are of the same gender, are the same age, and are given similar training posts. But Fanny feels that Cecilia has extra qualities (self-confidence and relational ease) that make all the difference. This difference makes Fanny feel she is not up to what is expected of her. Fanny focuses on the qualities she feels she does not possess. Cecilia is a reflection of Fanny, but a reflection that is distorted by the unbearable difference.

Here is what Fanny wrote a few months after her episode of envy: "This relationship affected me, destabilized me and reinforced my impression that my colleagues were hostile towards me [. . .]. My relationship with Cecilia was conditioned by my desire to do better than her, all the more so as Cecilia was an outgoing and dynamic person who adapted well and who easily interacted with others. At the beginning of the training course, I felt a lot of uncertainty about my future and feared that I would be compared to Cecilia, that I would work less efficiently than she did. I then started comparing myself to her, identifying with her and doubting my own choices [. . .]. In her presence I felt transparent, I felt I had no place there and that I had nothing to offer to anyone around me. For example, at the beginning of the training period, when we had lunch with other members of the team, I found it difficult to talk because she (Cecilia) had a tendency to push herself forward. [...] This difficult relationship consumed all my energy and as I withdrew into myself, it became an obstacle to my integration into the team. Preoccupied about my relationship with Cecilia, I did not interact with others and did not try to get to know them [...]. I was obsessed with this relationship [...] Indeed, even if I tried to ignore it, I felt this disquiet "gnaw" at me. And as time passed this relationship became more and more unbearable.

Not knowing how to handle the situation, I distanced myself. What is paradoxical is that during my assignments I tended to identify with her work, to follow her ideas and therefore I did not assert myself. [...] This process [...] reinforced my initial lack of self-confidence, causing me to doubt my choices and to feel worthless as a person. Moreover, I felt lost because I felt my missions and objectives were not clearly defined; I was afraid of the unknown and of the void and Cecilia was perhaps the solution. [...] For example, when we had to draw up analysis matrixes, I often "resigned" myself to using hers because I thought I was incapable of doing it as well as she did."

Doubting her own abilities, Fanny closes herself off and avoids interaction with her teammates for fear of being put in the wrong. She is afraid of taking initiatives and, fearing she will fail or make the wrong decisions, prefers to copy her training mate. This period is accompanied by emotional pain and depressive isolation. Fortunately, she eventually learns to look at her situation from a more distant perspective, and as a result, manages to evolve, take more initiatives, and become more autonomous. One of the factors that helped Fanny in this process was the fact that after a few months, the department in which both students were working went through organizational changes. This reorganization clearly separated the sports department, where Cecilia was working, from the gardening department, where Fanny was. Whereas, initially the two students were constantly "in each other's face" and had to work together, the reorganization of the departments separates them physically. Fanny no longer watches Cecilia's every move and no longer feels the need to compare herself – always unfavorably – to her. As Fanny later commented, she could then start *"rebuilding herself"*.

Hostility, aggressiveness, and destruction

Envious individuals sometimes act out the hostility and resentment they feel against the person they envy. Envy can then generate violence and aggression, the envious individuals wishing to destroy the object of envy, to deprive the envied of their perceived advantage or to sabotage his or her reputation. All these attempts are made in order to eliminate what is at the origin of envy and re-establish what the envious perceive as a fair balance between the envied and themselves.[16]

Aggression against the rival is a direct manifestation of envy that has been highlighted by some psychoanalysts. Indeed, the followers of Melanie Klein[17] have shown that envy arises very early in the psychological development of human beings and that it can lead to aggressive behaviors that are sometimes extremely destructive, including for the envious people themselves.

In organizations, aggressive behavior related to envy is a common phenomenon.[18] It is this specific symptom that generally reveals the presence of envy. This does not mean that aggressive behavior is the most frequent consequence of envy, but that the other consequences can be more difficult or even impossible to pinpoint, whereas aggressiveness and attack are more noticeable.

Harming the reputation of the envied person

Envious individuals can, to start with, be content with verbally attacking and belittling the people they envy, by harming their reputation, and by drawing attention to some of their limitations. The envious can even resort to slander in an attempt to destroy the integrity of the envied. In some cases, the attack on an envied individual's reputation is subtler.

Case 6: A biased committee[19]

In a New Zealand university, a particularly gifted young lecturer is unfairly assessed by an evaluation committee, some members of which are envious of her qualities. The committee must decide whether this young lecturer should be given tenure or not.

Instead of attacking her directly, the envious members of the committee exploit the ambiguity of certain evaluation rules in an attempt to influence the other members. They justify their rejection by giving a high priority to the criteria related to administrative responsibilities, and in so doing discard the exceptional academic qualities of the applicant as secondary. What is more, they intentionally undervalue the administrative work she has performed in the department, taking advantage of the fact that the members of the committee do not all have access to the relevant information.

This is a good example of disguised slander, where a few envious individuals, under cover of a supposedly objective evaluation procedure, harm another person's reputation.

In other cases, the attack is more direct. The philosopher Schopenhauer was well known for systematically trying to oust his rivals, particularly those who aspired to the title of Master. He had no qualms in belittling and criticizing the people he envied, even when they were recognized philosophers. When Hegel, then at the pinnacle of his fame, obtained a professorship at the University of Berlin (1820), Schopenhauer decided to schedule his lectures at the same time as his rival's most anticipated seminar. When the relevant department offered to reschedule his lectures, Schopenhauer preferred to resign from the university.[20] In such cases, not only is collaboration impossible, but the organization – in this particular instance the University of Berlin – also loses one of its most outstanding members; one that contributed to its prestige.

Envy and sabotage

Envy can also lead the envious to actions that are nothing short of sabotage. I have already discussed the example of the two departments that prevented the academic department from conducting their workshop in ideal conditions. Let us now look at the following example.

Case 7: **Latent sabotage**
Karine is a graduate from business school with a few years' working experience. She accepts a position as a purchasing agent in the marketing department of a distance-selling company. She works under the supervision of Martine, the supply and purchasing

director. The latter also works with an assistant: Caroline has a postgraduate diploma, is about the same age as Karine, and has been working in the company for several years.

Two weeks after Karine's arrival, Martine goes on maternity leave. It soon becomes clear that her post will not be filled and that, when she returns to work, Martine will be assigned a new position in a different department. For a few months the role distribution is unclear: will Martine's functions be assigned to another person? As the weeks pass, the management progressively entrusts Martine's missions to Karine, which, given her existing post and professional history, is an appropriate decision.

The moment this configuration becomes clear, Caroline's behavior changes. She undertakes a more or less latent form of sabotage, "forgetting" certain missions that Karine has given her, and keeping important information from the latter. Karine then finds out that when Martine announced she was pregnant, Caroline hoped that she would be given Martine's post. Yet Caroline's qualifications and her mostly administrative work experience (as a director's assistant) do not match what is needed to successfully perform Martine's functions. Karine then joins the company; her level of education is comparable with Caroline's, but thanks to the specific skills she was trained in, she is better suited than Caroline to the position in question. Thus, after only a few weeks, Karine is given what Caroline has been coveting. Caught in the grip of envy, the latter appears to have become hostile to Karine, wishing her harm and endangering her reputation by jeopardizing some of her missions, preventing her from achieving deadlines, etc. In so doing, Caroline jeopardizes her own job because her "mistakes" are seen a lack of professionalism. But she knows that through these "mistakes" she is harming Karine, and particularly her reputation.

Envy and destruction

When envy is very strong, it can really lead an envious individual to destroy the people they envy or what they possess. Many traditional tales illustrate this aspect of envy. Thus, the famous Judgment of Solomon depicts two women who have given birth. One of them loses her child and both women start fighting over the surviving infant, each claiming to be his mother. Called in to solve the dispute, King Solomon asks for a sword so as to cut the surviving infant in two and give each woman her share of the baby. One accepts, whereas the other refuses, preferring to give the baby away to the other woman rather than see him die. According to Solomon, this is a sign that she is the true mother of the child. As for the envious woman, her intentions are clear: deprive the mother of her child by killing him if need be. In Pushkin's "Mozart and Salieri",[21] the musician Salieri, envious of Mozart's exceptional talents, develops a plan to progressively wear him out and eventually kill him. In the Judeo-Christian tradition, Satan envies God, the creator of life, of the world and of all that exists. By bringing temptation, division, and conflict, Satan destroys the harmony and the perfection of the original creation.

But envious individuals can also engage in behaviors that have harmful consequences for themselves.[22] Findings in experimental economics[23] show that envious people might accept less than optimal monetary reward as long as another participant's advantage is reduced. This "burning the rich" comes at a financial cost for the envious too, but the envious is ready to behave in this manner if it means that "the rich get poorer". Envy can thus motivate people to act in ways that reduce the absolute level of their possible outcomes. In some cases, this means that they are prepared to destroy the system they, themselves, depend upon, if it also results in the destruction of the envied subject. This aspect is clearly apparent in the Gucci case described below.

Case 8: Gucci or mutual annihilation[24]

The Gucci affair is a striking example of destructive envy. Driven by envy, different members of the Gucci family, who were also shareholders in the company, spent enormous amounts of money suing one another for decades over legal disputes. Judge William C. Conner of the New York District Court compared the Gucci family feud to the biblical story of Abel and Cain, in which Cain, envious of his brother Abel whose offering God preferred to his, kills his brother.

Gucci was a family-owned firm founded in Florence at the turn of the 20th century, and which became one of the world's most successful fashion businesses. However, in the 1970s the firm started suffering the consequences of endless disputes between the brothers Aldo and Rodolpho Gucci – the controlling shareholders of the company – and their sons, Paolo and Maurizio respectively. From then on, fathers and sons, cousins, uncles and nephews, husbands and wives endlessly accused one another of tax evasion, illegal export of capital, fraud, attempted murder, etc. The members of this family seemed to have been more concerned with destroying each other's lives than enjoying their own. All this led them to spend enormous amounts of money in court cases – copiously covered by the international press – and eventually to sell their shares in the business, lose control of their firm and, for some, to spend a few years in jail.

"The tall poppy syndrome"

Another effect of envy is a phenomenon whereby some people modify their behavior in order to avoid being envied. Some individuals, gifted with above-average talents, can intentionally reduce their performance level, or not fully utilize their potential, so as to maintain good relations with their peers and avoid provoking envy and possible hostility.[25] This is called "tall poppy syndrome".[26] An Australian phrase, it is used to describe people's wish to harm so-called "tall poppies", namely people who are the target of envy because they are more successful than others. The heads of the tall poppies must be cut off so that they cannot become more than the average, and so that their abilities are more "normal" and therefore more acceptable.

An increasing staff turnover

Given all the symptoms discussed above, it is no wonder envy has a direct effect on the rate of turnover among members of work teams. Even the envious individuals themselves may leave. Indeed, their dissatisfaction with work and their bad relationships with their bosses can make them want to change jobs. They might also leave because they can no longer bear to face what has driven them to envy. Thus, Schopenhauer chose to leave the University of Berlin rather than have to face Hegel, his rival.

But the envied people too might decide to leave, to escape the hostility they are encountering, and to find a healthier working environment. They might decide to leave when the attacks against them have a long-term negative effect on them.[27] Thus, the young lecturer mentioned above sees her career prospects in the university diminished as a consequence of being unfairly evaluated. This leads her to resign and, as a result, the faculty loses its most promising member to a competing university.

Even when envy does not lead to aggression, it makes collaboration difficult and generates tensions, because the envious tend to dislike the envied, find it difficult to interact with the latter, and behave "strangely" towards them. In the case of the two students doing their on-the-job training in the same company, Cecilia notices that her relationship with Fanny, who envies her, is difficult and tense: the latter avoids her at times, imitates her at other times, and she is very sensitive to any remark made by her team members concerning the work accomplished by either Cecilia or herself. But Cecilia does not understand Fanny's behavior; she does not see that it is caused by envy and does not know how to react to her. Envied people generally do not understand why they are being attacked. Indeed, envious individuals seldom explain why they behave so aggressively, and in some cases might not even be aware of the reason themselves. As for the victims of this hostility, they are generally unable to identify envy as the cause of this behavior, and in some cases feel guilty and partly blame themselves for the relational difficulties that ensue. In short, the envied can feel uncomfortable in their work environments, and this, needless to say, does not exactly encourage them to stay.

Finally, the members of a team or organization in which envy is visibly present (even when they cannot associate the term "envy" with the symptoms they observe) are also more likely to leave their team because of the poor working atmosphere. All these factors therefore result in higher turnover rates and make it difficult to create stable and cohesive working teams.[28]

In view of the consequences of envy discussed so far, we could provisionally conclude that envy, when it occurs in the workplace, tends to have negative effects on teams, and more generally on organizations. However, we should not ignore the other, albeit rare, aspects mentioned at the beginning of this chapter, as they lead to a more nuanced portrait of envy.

Some paradoxical effects of envy in professional environments

The reproduction of the system

I have, thus far, talked about the potentially destructive effects of envy on organizations. However, for the sake of impartiality, it is important to mention one fundamental paradox of envy. Yes, envy can harm the system in which it develops, but it only occurs because the envious individuals adhere to the system that designates what, in the context, is of value and is desirable.[29]

What is of value and a source of advantage for the envied is dictated by a value system that encompasses both protagonists. By being envious, the envious individuals implicitly reaffirm their adherence to and dependence on this system, thus contributing to its reproduction. One of the paradoxical consequences of envy is, therefore, that it can seriously disrupt social systems because of the hostile behaviors it generates, while at the same time contributing to their stability by feeding the value system that rules them.

Envy leads to action

Admittedly, envy can, in some cases, act as a motivator and stimulate the envious person.[30]

This aspect of envy is mentioned by the anthropologist Foster,[31] in his fundamental paper on envy: "At the risk of oversimplification, I would say that man views envy phenomena along two distinct axes, which for lack of better terms can be called the competitive axis and the fear axis." According to him, envy falling along the competitive axis urges the individual to behave in a proactive way so as to attain specific goals such as "raise(ing) or secure(ing) one's status vis-à-vis the competitor or challenger". However, Foster does not develop this axis and focuses in his paper on the other axis – the fear axis, which is strongly related to the destructive side of envy.

As for workplace envy, it has been suggested that it could be a "catalytic" emotion,[32] likely to stimulate people and prompt action.[33] Envy can be quite dysfunctional but it can also be "functional in that it can energize behavior and act as a discriminative cue for eliciting coping response".[34] Some writers have suggested that envy may be a healthy prerequisite for leadership in organizations,[35] and a needed spur to ambition in a competitive market economy.[36]

Only one study has shown that envy could encourage envious people to improve their performances.[37] Thus, in the example of the Hong Kong branch of an international bank (Case 4), envy is related to the promotion of some employees and not others. On the one hand, among the candidates whose applications for promotion were rejected, those who admitted to being more envious than others of the employees who got promoted, were also those who, from the start, identified most with the successful candidates (in other words, they viewed themselves as comparable to the latter). On the other hand, and this is interesting, the envious individuals had higher performance rates than their less envious colleagues, five months after the promotions. Envy served as a stimulant and encouraged the envious people to improve. It led to emulation.

There is an interesting relationship between the two observations: the envious individuals are certainly envious partly because they consider themselves deserving, in so far as they view themselves as comparable to the employees who have been promoted. They therefore probably interpret the fact that the others have been promoted as evidence that they themselves can also win promotion: all they need do is improve their performance. In this example, the feeling of inferiority the envious individuals experience as a result of not getting promoted actually encourages them to improve their performance so as to prove that they are also capable of achieving. Instead of being paralyzed by failure, the envious have been stimulated and engage with renewed energy in the competition. As I emphasized in Chapter 1, envy can be associated with admiration for the envied, in the same way as it can be associated with hatred and resentment.[38] And admiration can lead to emulation, the envied individuals serving as models. This hypothesis, discussed further in Chapter 3, seems all the more relevant here as it can be related to another observation: envious subjects envy people with whom they feel comparable, people with whom they have many characteristics in common. Envied people are therefore models that can be imitated, goals that can be reached.

Case 9: **The promotion of a friend**[39]
A university lecturer hears that a colleague, who is also a friend, has been offered a sought-after post in a more prestigious university. At first, he is very surprised because he thought that, like

himself, his friend had for a long time given up his ambitious career plans and was content with a less prestigious post in a provincial university. He becomes envious of his friend, who suddenly distinguishes himself and acquires a new status. Then, with envy comes questioning: "Why not me? Couldn't I also obtain a position like his? Why did I give up my career plans?"

In this case, the feeling of envy awakens in the envious person's long-buried desires, which he thought he had long renounced. The sudden pain shows that his desires were not extinguished: like wind, envy fans the coals to life again.

The same man feels envious again later when he hears that his secretary has finally found a publisher for her book, whereas he has not written anything for many years. Thus, she is going to join the circle of writers he used to be part of, and once again he experiences, though this time with nostalgia, the excitement of that long gone era. He suddenly imagines himself writing a new book. He wonders: "Why not try again? Don't I also want to feel the thrill of those days again?"

Thus, envy can awaken the ability to delve into a new path, because the comparison with the *other,* which is at the foundation of envy, reveals new reference points and goals. This is the facet of envy, related to desire more than to hostility towards the envied, which prevails in this case. Envy can act as a powerful stimulant. What is essential in this process is the moment when the person becomes aware of feeling envious and asks him/herself if the gap between him/herself and another person that has suddenly revealed itself can be filled. It is important that self-esteem not be too damaged for the person to be able to engage in this type of process.

Envy or sense of morality?

Envy is associated with a feeling of injustice.[40] This feeling is thought to develop in order to enable envious people to re-establish a cognitive and emotional equilibrium, while avoiding damage to their self worth: "If the other succeeds or gets more or better than I do, it is not because he deserves it – for he and I are very alike – but because he is favored by an unjust system." The feeling of injustice is then a means of defense against the feeling of inferiority that results from an unfavorable comparison to the other person.

In organizations, individuals feel strongly about being equitably rewarded for what they do. This has an effect on their motivation, their loyalty towards their company, or their stability.[41] Equity is relative in so far as the employees' perceptions of it are based, to a large extent, on a comparison with other employees, and particularly with those with whom they have much in common in terms of function, workload, etc. Employees who collaborate together are sensitive not only to the reward and remuneration levels set by their organization for certain outputs (salaries, promotion, etc.) but also to the procedures governing the amount and distribution of the remuneration. The feeling of equity therefore implies a distributive justice (what is distributed) and a procedural justice (the rules that govern this distribution).

Thus, in organizational environments, individuals demand equity, and the feeling of unfairness can negatively affect their behavior. But where does this demand for fairness come from? What are its roots? Why are people in organizations so sensitive to injustice?

The sociologist Helmut Schoeck[42] raises the same question with respect to social systems and observes that many sociological and political theories have emphasized the fact that people in society demand equity, but have not explored the origins of this demand. According to Schoeck, however:

> Individuals are little concerned about equality; often their sense of justice rebels precisely because they are not granted the unequal treatment they believe they are entitled to [. . .] In the absolute, what matters for a worker is not the amount of his wage, but the difference between himself and the other workers. It is when the scale of wages does not reflect what he perceives as a difference between the difficulty or importance of his tasks and the difficulty or importance of the other workers' tasks, that most protests occur.

He explicitly designates envy as the origin of the demand for justice:[43] inequality is unbearable because the difference with the other triggers envy. But because envy is socially taboo, one way of keeping it under cover and at the same time modifying what generates it, is to refer to the need for justice and equity, which is socially valued. In this process, the aim is to turn a personal emotion into a collective protest.

Admittedly, the desire for equity and the sense of injustice is not systematically related to envy.[44] The relation exists when a person's sense of injustice appears to be "subjective"; that is, when an outside observer, after analyzing the differences between the envious and the envied, does not automatically attribute these differences to an unjust system, but to causes related to the qualities of the envied individuals or to their achievements (which are objectively higher). In this case, it is the envious people who interpret the differences as being caused by an injustice, which enables them to protect their self-esteem. As a result of this, the envious behave aggressively and with hostility towards those they envy. Experiments concerning this aspect of envy clearly show that it is only when envious individuals feel there has been an injustice[45] that they behave aggressively towards the people they envy.

Here again the ambiguity of envy is apparent. The desire of individuals in work environments for equity and justice is real, but is this desire the result of a true sense of morality or does it, in some cases, conceal envy? Supposing that envy is at the root of this desire requires a less naive and more complex exploration of the origins of certain "moral" preoccupations.

How are these paradoxical effects related?

We come to the end of this chapter and find ourselves puzzled. On the one hand, envy is associated with hatred, resentment, and to effects that can have serious consequences for organizational life: attacks against the envied, impact on workplace atmosphere and performance, a high turnover rate, demotivation. On the other hand, envy seems to have another, positive, albeit less studied, facet: it can stimulate the envious and encourage them to improve their performance; it can act as a driving force for action – which, in environments where action is highly valued, is not without significance – and it can help sustain the value system upon which any organization is built.

Why are such contradictory and paradoxical phenomena observed? In order to answer this question, in Chapter 3 we present one theory that explains the existence of processes underlying envy.

Card 2   Identifying the symptoms of envy in my team

Envy always hides beneath other dysfunctions, which makes it difficult to spot. Here are a few questions that you can ask yourself and which will help you see things more clearly. The more affirmative answers you give to these questions, the more likely it is that envy is at the root of what you observe. Reasoning in terms of envy will enable you to see the relation between seemingly unrelated problems:

- I often hear team members speak ill of their colleagues.
- When a success has been achieved we hear people say "it's thanks to X or Y" rather than "we all contributed to it".
- The people who do too well do not stay in my team.
- The members of my team constantly compare and evaluate one another.
- In practice, my colleagues find it difficult to work together on common projects.
- In my department, it is not uncommon for certain individuals to be pushed aside.
- My co-workers watch each other a lot.
- Where I work, there is a lot of withholding of information.
- There is no harmony in my team.
- There is a lot of discontent and dissatisfaction among my colleagues.
- Many people in my organization are sick of the system.
- Where I work, I always hear people complain that they are not recognized.
- When an unexpected problem arises in the team, it generates tension, rather than solidarity, between the team members.
- There is a lot of hostility between the people I work with.
- Many people complain about their manager because he never gives positive feedback.

3
Envy, Desire, and Mimetism

In this chapter, my discussion will be based, for the most part, on a thesis introduced in the 1960s and then further developed by René Girard, a renowned French philosopher whose work has been very influential, particularly in the United States where he teaches comparative literature. This thesis is known as the "theory of mimetism", the "mimesis theory" or "theory of mimetic desire".

René Girard and the theory of mimetic desire
René Girard's publications on the subject are too many to list here. Indeed, his thesis on "mimetic desire" and on the "mimesis theory" is discussed and developed throughout all his writings.

To those interested, I would suggest they start with his first book *Deceit, Desire and the Novel: Self and Other in Literary Structure* (1965), in which he states his theory, by dissecting the mechanism of desire. In this book, which constitutes the theoretical foundation of his approach, he uses his analysis of some literary masterpieces as a basis for developing his theory. In *Violence and the Sacred* (1977), he uses Greek Tragedy as a basis for understanding the origins of violence in human society, which he attributes to the infernal spiral of mimetic desire, which produces evenness and destroys differences. Designating a victim, who is then turned into a scapegoat, enables people to solve the crisis by displacing the violence onto the outsider (the scapegoat), which then enables the community to unify in violent unanimity. Girard develops these hypotheses further in *To Double Business Bound: Essays on Literature, Mimesis and Anthropology* (1978), *The scapegoat*

(1986) and *Job: the victim of his people* (1987). In *A theater of envy: William Shakespeare* (1991), he offers an outstanding analysis of some of the famous playwright's works. According to him Shakespeare clearly set out the principle of mimetic desire in some of his plays, but concealed his knowledge of this principle in his subsequent works.

I shall discuss his theory of desire and of envy, but will leave aside his theory of religions and most of his reflections on the resolution of the mimetic crisis through scapegoating.

The classic conception: autonomous in one's desire

As mentioned earlier, underlying envy is desire: an envious person desires something he/she does not have and which another person has managed to obtain. But why does the envious person desire this particular thing rather than another? What bonds him/her to this object (a resource, a good, a promotion, a person, etc.)?

The conventional approach, both in social sciences and common sense, starts with a subject–object couple: human beings focus their desire on objects featuring characteristics that are more or less valued by their system of preferences. The desire I have for a man, a job, or a garment is supposed to result from my personal choice: I choose, at a given time, to focus my desire on such and such an "object of desire". In this perspective, each object has a quality that has the ability to attract my desire. Each object is supposed to have an intrinsic value, in relation to my preferences, to my tastes and to the norms that govern me, etc. Whether this so-called "choice" really results from free will or is actually influenced by an unconscious impulse or social norms does not seem to matter: in all these theories, the subject–object couple has its own autonomy.

A motivation that is independent of others

In the field of management, almost all the theories about motivation are also based on the hypothesis of an autonomous subject–object couple. The most used theory is that known as Maslow's Theory.[1]

Maslow's Theory

Each individual is thought to be motivated by increasingly complex and hierarchically ordered needs. Thus, in order of priority we have: physiological needs, safety needs, social needs, esteem needs and finally self-actualization needs. Once the lower level needs are satisfied (safety for example), individuals move up to the next level of needs and so on until they reach the personal devel-opment level.

This famous theory is frequently used to study motivation in the workplace. Yet Maslow's work is usually interpreted so simplistically that the so-called "Maslow's theory" bears little relation to this author's writings.

It is this theory, or rather the way it is usually interpreted in management manuals, that we shall discuss here, because it is representative of how management theories oversimplify the mechanisms of motivation.

Though this theory has been criticized, it continues to be taught. Even more surprising is the fact that Maslow's critics have not questioned the validity of the hypothesis that individuals are autonomous in their motivational processes, and isolated from the processes of others.

More generally, this hypothesis is found in all the motivation theories that seek to determine what, in organizations, drives individuals to action. Some draw attention to the nature and content of the work individuals are expected to perform, which according to these theories are determining factors.[2] Others focus on the needs of individuals.[3] Others still are based on the hypothesis that individuals adjust their behavior at work according to their perceived probability of getting a reward.[4]

One exception: the theory of equity

To my knowledge, only one theory of motivation has introduced the idea that individuals could compare themselves to others. It is the equity theory.[5] It postulates that workers' motivation is determined by their work satisfaction, which in turn depends on their perceptions of how equitable their company is. The sense of equity is related to the employees' perceptions of the ratio between what they feel they put into their job (input) and what they get in return (output). To assess whether this ratio is fair, the workers need a benchmark. So they look at what the other employees "receive" from their employers in return for what they "give", so as to determine whether the input/output ratios of those other employees are identical to their own. If the workers perceive that there is a difference, they will tend to:

- either modify their perception of that difference. For example, if they feel that other employees receive proportionately more than they do in relation to what they put in, they might try and find reasons to justify this difference. They might tell themselves that the other employees have worked in more difficult working conditions than they have, and therefore have expended more energy;
- or modify their own behavior in order to restore a sense of equity. They might decide to work less if they feel that what they get in return for what they put into their job is insufficient compared to what others get.

Thus, the equity theory does refer to social comparison, in so far as it postulates that people determine whether the ratio between what they get from their employer and what they give is equitable or not by comparing this ratio to that of other individuals; but this reference to comparison is superficial.

Firstly, people need reference points in order to assess in a sufficiently "rational" and objective manner whether what they get for their efforts is fair or unfair. The unpleasant feeling people may experience merely results from the cognitive realization that there is a gap between themselves and others; and the hypothesis is that these people seek to cancel this difference either by modifying their behavior (for example, by working less in order to restore a balance between what they feel they put in and what they receive, in relation to other employees) or by modifying their perception (by convincing themselves that such and such an employee, whom they believe is proportionately better paid than they are, actually has a more difficult job than they do, or is more senior, which justifies the gap between them). In this case, people are supposed to behave in a very rational and detached way.

Secondly, the "Other" this theory refers to can also be the individual him or herself ("Person"), but in a different context: "Other is usually a different individual, but may be Person in another job or in another social role. Thus, Other might be Person in a job he held previously, in which case he might compare his present and past outcomes and inputs and determine whether or not the exchange with his employer, present or past, was equitable."[6] If the "Other" is the person him or herself, the process cannot be defined as a social comparison.

The hypothesis of mimetic desire

This is where René Girard's theory becomes useful. Through his analyses of some literary masterpieces, he developed a problematic of desire that differed vastly from that which had been accepted until then. According to Girard, the common conception of desire, though it gives us a sense that we are free and autonomous in our choices, is nonetheless invalid.[7] What he puts forward is the mimetic aspect of desire: men imitate one another and the desire of one man is nothing but the other's desire. We only desire the things that others designate as desirable. Here, Girard substitutes the subject–object couple for a triangular relationship between the subject, the object, and the other, in which the subject imitates the desire of the other, who then plays the role of mediator between the subject and the object.

Fascinated by the other's desire

Let us take as an example the story told by New York painter Paul Jenkins about his friend Mark Rothko, a master of American contemporary art, at a time when the latter had not yet acquired his reputation as a major artist.

> **Case 10: "Give me my painting back"**
> At the time, Paul Jenkins had his studio a block away from Mark Rothko's, and both artists used to visit each other regularly to discuss art together. Paul Jenkins recalls that "During a visit to his studio in 1956, I became entranced by a small painting and told Mark I wanted to buy it. He accepted my offer and then walked home with me, and with the painting under his arm. Then the next day and in an agitated state, Mark called me to say that he needed to have the painting back and that he would keep my check but not cash it. I know that it meant something to Mark that I wanted this painting so much. He told that to a friend, who later told me."[8]

From this account it seems that his friend and colleague's enthusiasm for the painting suddenly made the latter so desirable in Mark Rothko's eyes that he could no longer let it go.

What does the conception of desire as mimetic imply in terms of envy? In the classical approach to desire, in which the subject is considered "autonomous", the cause of the emergence of envy lies in the object of desire: the subject desires the object; the other possesses it; envy therefore targets whoever appears as an obstacle between the subject and the object. It is seen as a consequence of the rarity of the object and of the coincidence by which several individuals are drawn to the same object.[9] If individuals operate in context where resources are abundant, or if these individuals choose different objects, then there is no reason for envy to emerge.

According to René Girard, this conception obscures the true reason for rivalry and envy. It is not so much the object that fascinates the subject, but the other. The subject desires the object because the other, whom he/she copies, desires it or sees it as desirable. In this context, the object in itself is not that important. This mechanism is particularly apparent in advertising:[10] In advertisements, the emphasis is placed not so much on the objective characteristics of products, but on the type of people who desire those products and who rejoice in possessing them. The potential consumer is invited to acquire a product that other people designate as desirable. Any object which other people possess and which the subject does not is likely to become desirable purely because others seem to desire it.

From imitation to violence

Thus, the subject imitates the other, or more precisely, the other's desire: in doing so, the subject uses the other as a model. But through a perverse process and by coveting the same object, the subject turns his/her model into a rival. This is how the conditions for a spiral of violence are created. Girard shows that primitive societies have an implicit understanding of these mechanisms and try to eliminate anything that might promote mimetism so as to prevent the violence that might come with it. Thus, revenge, which is a repetition of the initial act of aggression, is condemned, and twins are separated or even killed. According to Girard, social rules and prohibitions are aimed at maintaining the separation and differences between people.

This thesis helps us to understand what imitation leads to. Learning specialists have for a long time known that imitation plays a fundamental part in the development of human beings, particularly of infants and children: it is because human children imitate the people around them that they are capable of progressively acquiring a number of motor and linguistic skills. But Girard's contribution has been to show that violence is an unavoidable consequence of imitation. The conflictual dimension is the other facet of imitation.

Mimesis, envy, and rivalry

Model and rival, rival because model

Two forms of mimesis can be distinguished:

- The case where the subject and the other play the roles of disciple and master respectively, and are aware of playing those roles;
- The case where, on the contrary, the subject and the other play very similar role and are comparable to each other.

The more "alike" the subject and the other are, the more imitation will cause the subject to turn his/her model into a rival, until eventually the subject becomes incapable of seeing the other as anything other than a rival. And as it is the other who is still in possession of the object, the subject responds to the question "Why does he/she have it, and not me?" by bringing to the fore the superiority of the rival. He/she is then incapable of freeing him/herself from his/her feeling of inferiority and this is where envy really stems from.

Thus, envy implies an extremely complex and painful relationship with the other: on the one hand, by dictating what is desirable the other introduces another intolerable dimension: a sense of lack. The subject becomes aware of what he/she desires and of the fact that he/she does not possess what he/she desires. It is therefore the other, and not the object itself, who is at the origin of envy. The object is but a pretext for envy to develop and masks the true reason for envy. On the other hand, envy comes with contradictory feelings; indeed the person the subject uses as a model unavoidably becomes his/her rival.

Admiration and hatred co-exist in the heart of envy:

The subject is torn between two opposite feelings toward his model – the most submissive reverence and the most intense malice. This is the passion we call "hatred". Only someone who prevents us from satisfying a desire that he himself has inspired in us is truly an object of hatred. The person who hates first hates himself for the secret admiration concealed by his hatred. In an effort to hide this desperate admiration from others, and from himself, he no longer wants to see in his mediator anything but an obstacle. The secondary role of the mediator thus becomes primary, concealing his original function of a model scrupulously imitated.[11]

Double mimesis and the spiral of violence

In this process, the relationship between the subject and the other becomes so paramount that the object disappears. As a result of this, a double process of mutual imitation can occur.

Indeed, the model is also a subject; as such he/she has to desire something and waits to be shown what is desirable. That is what the first subject of the subject–model–object triangle does: the subject's desire for the object transforms the latter and gives it particular value. This causes the object to become either truly desirable, or even more desirable for the model. The latter needs to have other desires in order to feel comforted in his/her desire for the object; he/she therefore enters a game of rivalry. Thus is unleashed a spiral of mimesis in which subject or model contribute to the emergence of the other as a rival. The infernal cycle of the mimetic process is now well established: no decrease in the desire of one will now escape the other's attention and the object will become more and more important in the resulting endless rivalry. We now have an infernal machine powered by the escalation of desire.

Let us take the example of the triangle formed by Mr de Rênal, Julien Sorel and Mr Valenod in Stendhal's novel *Le Rouge et le Noir*.[12]

Case 11: **Who will have Julien Sorel?**

Monsieur de Rênal is a gentleman and the mayor of a small French town, Verrières. He is considering hiring the young Julien Sorel as a tutor for his children. Why? As Stendhal implies, the reason seems to be the following: Monsieur de Rênal thinks that Valenod, an unscrupulous and wealthy bourgeois, has the same idea.

Later on in the novel, Valenod does indeed make a proposition to Julien Sorel to that effect. But this only superficially confirms M. de Rênal's intuition. Valenod, because of his apparent wealth and status in the town, becomes M. de Rênal's object of obsession. The latter uses Valenod as a model and seeks to know what the latter desires so as to acquire his object of desire before he does. He believes that Valenod wishes to employ Julien Sorel as a tutor and starts desiring the same thing. In doing so, he shows his model, who has now become his rival, what the object of their rivalry is. Valenod then expresses his desire for what de Rênal desires, which is nothing other than what the latter believes is Valenod's object of desire.

The initial illusion becomes reality in an endless mimetic spiral in which, in turns, each man imitates what he believes is the other's desire. The object escapes both and no longer has any reality, and is obliterated in the spiral of mutual imitation. The object itself is nothing but a pretext to fuel the cycle of mutual imitation. Naturally, a person standing outside this mimetic triangle, one who is not overpowered by illusion, would wonder: "What is it, in this object, that they find so desirable?" But, once trapped in the triangle, the subject will never admit that his rival is also his model; similarly, the model will never admit that the subject is his rival, and the object becomes the object of desire of both the subject and the model, and has become indispensable to both.

The subject is not aware of the mimetic process and continues to believe that he/she desires the object because of its intrinsic qualities: "Rivalry itself reinforces this illusion. The antagonists are convinced that a major difference separates them, a difference without which they would not oppose each other. They cannot imagine that their difference is rooted in their alikeness. The apparent and deceiving primacy of the object persuades each rival to be the victim of the other."[13]

But, though Girard presents this mechanism as one that occurs quite systematically, observation of reality leads us to a more nuanced conclusion. Thus, in the above example of the painting bought by Paul Jenkins, the latter accepted to give the object back despite the intensity of his desire for it. He could have wanted to keep it at all costs, as the painting became all the more desirable as Rothko wanted to have it back; this could have led them both into the mimetic spiral and cycle of violence described above. Jenkins's strong friendship for Rothko and his desire to protect this relationship prevailed over his desire for the painting. Nevertheless, the fact that he told the story in 2005, almost half a century after the incident occurred, is an indication of the effect it had on him and of how difficult it must have been for him to part with the painting.

A difficult acknowledgment

Why is it so difficult to admit that at the root of envy lies a mimetic desire? First of all, because this would mean accepting that our desires are seldom our own and that the energy we invest in acquiring certain things (promotion, status, goods, etc.) is not justified by their intrinsic value. We intensely desire things, not for what they intrinsically are, but because we are under the impression that an *other* points them out as desirable. This approach shatters the contemporary but idealistic belief that people are autonomous in their desires and their ability to choose. People are seen as desiring subjects, who as such are haunted by a sense of lack, but who do not actually know what they desire. In their wandering search, they come across others who possess something they themselves do not have, and which seems to endow these persons with a completeness of which they themselves are deprived. This apparent completeness fascinates the subject and awakens the haunting question "what do you have that I don't have?" (and that got you your beautiful car, your job, or your happiness). The boundary between the self and others is much more porous than generally envisaged.

The second reason is, without a doubt, related to the fact that acknowledging the importance of the mimetic processes amounts to acknowledging the precedence of the model, which in turn comes down to admitting to one's own feeling of incompleteness and inferiority. The envious is fascinated by the other and by his or her status.

More fundamentally, perhaps, admitting that our desire partly originates in our imitation of an other, would force us to accept the resulting consequences (mentioned above): the people we use as models are also the people we hate; it is because we admire them that we end up hating them! This is enough to drive anyone mad. Incapable of recognizing the other as being simultaneously the model and the rival, the subject constantly wavers between the two.

This is undoubtedly why envy is such a painful and destabilizing emotion: it brings into play many dimensions that are potentially contradictory and yet interlinked in a process envious subjects are incapable of detecting because they can never identify its origin – the fact that they desire something because they believe that another person also wants that thing.

A new look at the cases of envy, from the perspective of the mimesis theory

The merit of the theory I have just outlined is essentially that it enables us to relate the seemingly different and contradictory phenomena described in Chapter 2.

Let us sum up what we have learnt so far: envy occurs between peers and arises in the framework of spheres of interest or activities that are important to the envious in terms of self-identity. Indeed, it is in relation to these spheres of interest that the envious rest on models with which they feel similar and imitate (we can call this identification). By imitating the other, they necessarily desire what they believe others point to as desirable. The models become the rivals and the envious are going to interpret the fact that they do not have that "something", which the models have, as a result of their own limitations. Envy is therefore associated with contradictory feelings of admiration and hatred toward the other and with a feeling of inferiority. Envious people are caused to compete with those they envy; this might encourage them to increase their performance or might, on the contrary, produce an overwhelming feeling of inferiority. In some cases, rather than trying to acquire the "others' objects of desire", the envious may attempt to deprive their rivals of those objects as a way of restoring "equality" between the envied and themselves. But the attacks of the envious against the envied can also be the simple consequence of the former's hatred for the latter.

Stimulated by the rival

Let us look again at the Hong Kong bank example. Among the candidates who were not promoted, those who admitted to being more envious than others of the employees who did win promotion also started liking the latter less and less once the names of the successful applicants were released. The envious employees were also those

who, from the start, identified most with the people who were promoted; it was also found that, five months after the promotion
process was completed, those envious employees had achieved
higher performance rates than their less envious colleagues.[14]
Girard's theory provides a useful explicative framework here. The
envied individuals are those the envious identify with the most:
those who serve as models for the envious. The envious people feel
hatred or hostility toward the individuals who have become their
rivals (but who were not before). At the same time, what the others
have obtained becomes even more desirable for the envious individuals and they will do anything to obtain it (in this case, a promotion –
the envious individuals strive to improve their performance so as to
have a better chance of being promoted in future), unlike the
employees who did not identify with and were not envious of those
who were promoted.

Friend and rival

Another example of mimetic desire in envy is provided in the case of
the professor who discovers that his colleague and friend has
obtained a post in a better university and feels envious as a result. In
this case, envy leads the professor in question to start wondering if
he too could progress in his career. In Chapter 2, I interpreted this as
a re-emergence of old desires. But it might also be that his colleague
pointed out to his envious friend what he was supposed to desire
(a better job and progress in his career). The professor might in the
past have wanted to progress in his career; however, but he could
have interpreted the fact that his colleagues were seemingly happy to
stay in this provincial university as a sign that teaching in this less
prestigious institution and therefore leading a stress-free life was
what was desirable. But suddenly, his friend upsets this balance by
showing him another object of desire. It is precisely because the professor closely identifies with his friend that he heeds this desire and
starts imagining himself looking for a better job.

Annihilated by the heroes

Finally, let us re-examine the case of the "Winning Factor" program,
the first effect of which was to designate some people as "heroes" and
as models that should be copied. These heroes obtain recognition
from the management team, whereas the employees whose efforts

are not acknowledged feel less valued than those who have been placed on a pedestal. The colleagues who once were their peers have now become their models, and from then on envy develops within the system. In this case, envy does not result in improved performance by the employees who are not appreciated: indeed, the distance which now separates the "heroes" from the others certainly feels too great and too unreal to stimulate the latter. On the contrary, what does take place is a general disengagement. Here, envy does not produce rivalry but self-withdrawal.

An ambiguous relation to the other

In the cases of workplace envy described in Chapter 2, we paid particular attention to the destructive side of envy. Here, envy results in the dissolution of the consulting agency founded by John and Peter; and a young lecturer is denied tenure by the evaluation committee. In each case, however, the envious party might feel both admiration and hatred towards the envied party, towards the model and rival; the envious individuals might also experience a feeling of inferiority related to their desire to do better.

Herein lies the ambiguity of envy: considering it occurs in relationships in which the "others" are models, is it not also what drives us to action? Isn't envy a factor of development as much as a poison? Isn't a child's development partly based on envy? When a mother says to her child, "Look, your brother can tie his shoelaces by himself. Soon you'll be able to do it too", doesn't she implicitly exploit envy to encourage her child to make progress? The child might envy her brother, but she also knows that she will eventually be able to be like him. The model helps progress, but is also at risk of becoming the rival. What is important is to prevent the rivalry from turning into an unmanageable spiral of violence.

For organizations, the problem seems to lie here: if, as a means of increasing performance rates, management systems exploit processes that unleash envy, they also run the risk of triggering a cycle of violence that will have serious consequences for the system. It is therefore critical to be aware of the contradictory effects of envy and to understand the potential consequences of such management systems. This is what we shall discuss in the following chapter.

4
How Management Systems Produce Envy

As I explained earlier, this book is not about envy as a pathological condition or as a strong personality trait. What I am interested in is envy as a fundamentally human emotion that most people are likely to experience in the workplace. René Girard shows that the function of traditional social systems is to prevent envy from becoming widespread and from degenerating into uncontrollable violence, which would put the system at risk of imploding (this function is always concealed from the group members and acts without their knowing). Thus, the mimesis theory does not envisage imitation as an automatic process; it is seen as a process that is intrinsic to the behavior of human beings living in groups, but one that the system can control.

My intention in this chapter is to understand what in organizational systems and management practices promotes envy and, above all, what contributes to keeping it either silent and inactive, or, on the contrary, causes it to escalate into violence. The problem with envy in an organization is not so much that it exists in the first place, for it is inherent to the behavior of individuals in a group, particularly in environments in which individuals are the object of comparison and evaluation (which is a fundamental characteristic of most organizations). The problem, I believe, is more that some systems allow envy to become a central component of their functioning, at the risk of letting it degenerate into a destructive spiral of violence.

There is another risk associated with envy in organizations: a temptation to resort to archaic management methods as a means of channeling envy. The challenge therefore consists of accepting the existence of envy, for it is inherent to the functioning of most organizations, while preventing it from causing too much damage.

To understand how organizational systems and management practices can cause envy to develop within organizations, I shall draw from sociological and anthropological studies of a number of communities that are organized in such a way as to better manage the problem of envy and prevent it from destroying the group. I will also use examples of envy in the workplace that I have observed.

The equalitarian utopia[1]

The most serious mistake that can be made about envy is to believe that it can be eradicated from firms, and more generally from organizations.

Indeed, one could easily think that by making all members of a group equal, and by eliminating all differences between them, there would no longer be any reason to become envious. Admittedly, envy is never recognized as the origin of the egalitarian demand, a demand that is based, rather, on the concept of struggle against inequalities and for justice. The general idea of egalitarianism is that most social problems would be solved if men lived in perfect equality. Despite the practical difficulties that the implementation of this egalitarian utopia presents, some collectivist societies – kibbutzim[2] in particular – have tried to apply its principles.

Case 12: **Kibbutzim**

Kibbutzim are communal Israeli settlements. The members of these communal villages choose to live according to strictly enforced socialist principles. Kibbutzim are intended to promote communal living in its ultimate form, by enforcing the principle of equality between its members, members who commit to do everything they can to remain equal. The application of this principle has in some cases been taken to an extreme: there were times when, in some kibbutzim, work clothes and underwear could not be personal items and had to be shared; they were washed in the communal laundry and then distributed. This overly strict rule was subsequently abandoned, but it is indicative of how far a community is prepared to go to ensure that equality applies to each and every aspect of daily life. This translates into the elimination of all economic and material inequalities, into an organization with no hierarchy of positions, no set division of labor, and in which no one is mandated with permanent authority, as authority rests with the collective rather than the individual.

These communities have been in operation for many years and continue to function in accordance with their founding principles. They therefore are fertile ground for observation for anyone trying to find out more about the effects of organizational structures and management systems on envy: has any community ever managed to create an environment in which there is no envy whatsoever? How do people who have lived in such communities since they were born, and have therefore been protected from the influences of individualism, behave? The answers are clear: in these communities, the problem of envy has neither been solved nor eliminated.

Banning envy

Firstly, setting up a rule that says "you shall not become different from the others, you must remain equal to the others" leads to a lack of innovation and to inertia, because of the feeling of guilt experienced by people who distinguish themselves from the others. Personal initiative is inhibited by the feelings of guilt experienced by individuals when they create a real or imagined difference. Everything is done to avoid making other people envious. Shame hangs over whoever proves more imaginative or bright than the others and is therefore no longer equal to the others. Personal intellectual activities are discouraged: intellectuals, who by definition engage in personal reflection, claim ownership of their ideas and clearly distinguish themselves from the others, and in doing so run counter to the ideal of equality.

Some studies have shown that similar phenomena occurred in popular revolutions. In many cases, intellectuals have been the victims of violent attacks, simply because they knew more than others or asserted their individuality. During the Chinese Cultural Revolution, for example, envy was clearly the root of the extreme violence to which intellectuals were subjected.[3]

The second lesson that can be drawn from the example of kibbutzim is that, in this type of organization, envy is not eliminated despite all the measures implemented to promote equality between all individuals. In an environment in which everything is done to ensure that individuals are all "alike", any minor difference gets blown out of proportion. Anything can then serve as a pretext for envy: different tastes, a different hobby, an achievement. This is where Girard's theory becomes useful: the more comparable and alike individuals are, the more permanent comparison is facilitated and the worse the effects of mimetism are. Furthermore, the communal ideology, by promoting conformity, reinforces the idea that if one subject desires one object, then all other subjects will desire it too.

The fundamental error in the egalitarian ideology lies in its very conception of what causes envy. Believing that absolute equality between people and the equal distribution of everything (meant in its widest sense) among them eliminate envy, boils down, once again, to believing that envy has its roots in the intrinsic characteristics and the rarity of the object. According to this approach, if all individuals possess exactly the same things in equal quantities, they no longer have any reason to envy others. But it is, and always is, the other who is the root of envy. The other can always be perceived as having a characteristic which he/she alone possesses, and which, through the effect of mimesis, reveals to the subject his/her own lack and his/her desire to acquire this "extra" quality. An equalitarian system in which comparison between individuals is permanent generates an environment in which the slightest differences are likely to be blown out of proportion.

Fear of envy and death of the group

If we apply these observations to organizations, we can make the following hypothesis: implementing an organizational policy based on an egalitarian principle and applied to every single aspect of organizational life would have disastrous consequences for the organization in terms of innovation and productivity, and in terms of its ability to evolve – because of the generalized fear of being envied. What is more, the organization would fail to eliminate envy. It would, in actual fact, facilitate its development. The prevalence of envy and of the fear of being envied would create a regressive organization, devoid of dynamism and riddled with more or less latent violence.

Admittedly, the strict principles of egalitarianism that govern every aspect of life in a kibbutz are unlikely to be applied in any other types of organization in the western world. But this is not to say that less extreme versions of egalitarianism cannot be found either. Let us examine the following case.[4]

Case 13: The group and the fantasy of equality

A group of people belonging to different organizations wishes to discuss the changes that have occurred in their field of competence and share their practices with one another. Most of them are university professors.

The first meetings are fruitful and rich in sharing. Soon, the members start thinking that the ideas generated during the meetings could serve as a basis to "produce" something. The production in question may take different forms: participation in conferences, the publication of a co-written book, etc. Some members of the group insist that the ideas generated by the group as a whole should not be used in individual productions. The knowledge produced during the group sessions belongs to the group and not to individuals. There seems to be some kind of fantasmatic or primitive fear that the group will be deprived of its food if the individuals use the ideas it has produced in other contexts.

The demand that the knowledge generated by the group be kept within the latter is, in fact, unrealistic. Indeed, all the members are engaged in their own personal research and because research is a long-term process, there can be no guarantee that what a member produces outside the group is not at least partly related to the work done by the group. As underlined earlier, one characteristic of the intellectual process is that the ideas it generates are eventually expressed in one's own personal way at some time or other during that process. This implies that the group cannot be a fusion of individuals in which the latter would be indissociably linked to and dependent on one another, and that, as a result, a process of differentiation is inevitable. This also implies that the contributions of each member to the collective process can take different forms. Finally, one must accept the fact that envy might emerge when, for example, it becomes clear that some of the members are more successful than others in using and developing their ideas outside the group.

The principles of equality and solidarity that seem to govern this group actually serve to mask the fear of envy. But they eventually lead to the death of the group: some of the members stop attending for fear of being accused of using the group's ideas in their own works, suspicion arises, and the session discussions become less and less productive. The fear of being envied hampers innovation. The group sticks to its archaic ways in the vain hope of keeping envy at bay. The fantasy that prevails in the group is that all members are identical to one another and contribute in an equal manner to the collective production. And yet, in an apparent paradox, envy still dwells, if only latently, within the group because some members keep a close watch on the others in an inevitably vain attempt to keep them from distinguishing themselves from the others. The group broke up quite soon after the question of "collective production" was raised.

To conclude this section, we can say that envy can, indeed, have negative consequences, but that the measures implemented to inhibit it can, in some cases, severely affect the development of the system and have effects that run counter to what was intended initially (and often unconsciously).

Generalized envy and violence as a means of motivation

As we have already established, envy stems from a very human tendency to desire what we think other people point to us as desirable, and in the process turning those people into our rivals. Envy is therefore likely to be associated with admiration and hatred for the model/rival. What is more, as an effect of mutual mimesis, the closer in similarity we become to our rivals and show them what we desire, the more determined they are to hang on to what they possess.

For organizations, and particularly contemporary firms whose management practices seek to constantly stimulate their staff into a never-ending performance race, exploiting envy in order to induce employees to improve their productivity and constantly strive for better results might appear to make sense. However, intentionally playing the envy card in order to leverage action presents enormous risks.

In Chapter 2, I discussed cases in which envy was a consequence of certain situations or management practices; but in these particular cases the management staff were not aware of envy and of its consequences on the teams. Thus, in the "Winning Factor" program, the airport's managers were convinced they were doing the right thing by publicly praising and rewarding certain employees, and it did not occur to them that these practices might generate envy.

In other firms or groups, however, envy is deliberately exploited as a means of stimulating individual performance, and is made part and parcel of the system. Let us now examine the case of a retail group we shall call Punchy.[5]

Case 14: Stimulating the sales force

Punchy is a chain of stores specializing in electrical household appliances (televisions, hi-fi, household equipment, multimedia appliances). The group has stores throughout France. We have concentrated on one store in particular, located in northern France and employing about 30 people managed by a director and a sales supervisor.

In this store, the salespeople are essentially paid on commission. The latter is determined according to the turnover of the store and the profit margin for each product sold. In order to motivate the sales force, contests and general competition are organized at the chain level. The salespeople employed in the different stores of the region are therefore frequently put in a position of competition against one another. In these contests the main goal is to sell as many items as possible (number of new products sold, number of obsolete products sold, etc.). The performances are calculated in proportion to the number of hours each employee works.

Thus, all employees can take part in these contests, regardless of whether they work part or full time, are employed under open or fixed term contracts, or are trainees or not. The results are calculated on a regular basis and disclosed once a month. The top three sales agents receive financial rewards varying between 150 Euros for the top agent, 90 Euros for the runner-up, and 60 Euros for third place (in the region). The management teams of all the stores are formally required to use this type of contest as a motivational tool for the sales force.

In the particular store we have studied, the director has intensified these practices and believes they are efficient motivational tools. Often on Saturdays, which are busy days, he organizes additional contests in which the winning sales agents can get a bottle of champagne, gift vouchers, or a CD depending on the sales made during the day. He also uses this type of incentive for special events such as Mother's Day. Furthermore, the sales agents are rated each day according to the sales they have made; the classification, which is displayed the following day, lists all the sales agents from the one with the highest rating to the one with the lowest. The word "top", "second", or "third" is written opposite the names of the top three agents of the day, and the word "last" is written opposite the name of the agent with the lowest rating. A comment is added to each result: *"Awake at last!"*, *"Don't forget the guarantees"*, *"See guys? That's how you must work!"* Sarcastic comments, such as *"That's just great, carry on"*, can also be added opposite the name of the lowest ranking agent. According to the director, this type of comment is used to "taunt the pride" of the sales agents concerned, to awaken their competitive spirit, and to "use the pride" of the sales staff to increase their daily performance. This daily comparison of results is also made during individual interviews; the director openly compares the person he is interviewing with another person. Most of the practices used by the manager of this store are used in other stores.

The store is divided into departments and sections, and each sales agent is normally assigned to one, priority, department. However, because the goal is to "make more sales", the agents can also work in sections that are not in their areas of expertise. The situation reaches its peak with the arrival of a new saleswoman who previously worked in another store of the chain and who has the ability to sell any type of product in any section of the store. Nicknamed "The Killer" by her colleagues and the management, her presence is appreciated by the management team "because the other sales agents will have to work hard to maintain their level and, mostly, they are going to have to go to the customers and offer their assistance more quickly because [. . .] they can no longer hide behind a protective monopoly". "They're going to have to put themselves out there; she's a 'killer' and she hasn't come here to make friends."[6]

In this environment, there is constant rivalry between the agents. The latter seem to readily take part in this internal competition. They carefully read the lists displayed daily and the results of the regional contests through which they can compare their own results to those of other agents both in their store and in others. It is not unusual for an agent who scored the lowest one day to score the highest the following day. Thus, one agent was heard saying: "See that! I finished last again yesterday. I'm gonna make a killing today, [. . .] I'm gonna show them!"

On the whole, the store achieves good results in terms of turnover and profit. However, the negative effects of these practices are far from negligible. Clashes between the employees are frequent. Fights erupt daily, often in front of customers. In some cases, the latter are even asked to take sides, in particular when they are about to sign an order form or when they start asking questions of someone other than the salesperson with whom they initially dealt. The employees often accuse one another of "stealing their leads" (to sell a product to a customer who had previously been assisted by another employee) or "stealing their customers". These clashes can degenerate into verbal insults and threats, often in front of the customers. The director systematically refuses to interfere in these conflicts, even when he is asked to take sides. He considers that "tension between the employees is always a good thing; it's better to let them have a go at each other; it forces them to fight for themselves and to move their [backsides]".

The relationships between the staff members seriously deteriorate: some, as a result of a fight, have not spoken to each other for months. The working environment is unpleasant. Not only is there no solidarity between the salespeople, but some of them resort to actions that verge on sabotage. For example, when an employee is told that a delivery has been canceled, he/she "omits" to inform the colleague who made the sale, which has repercussions on the customers. More generally, the customers, apart from having to witness the fights between the sales agents, can end up being accused by a salesperson of not understanding that he is paid on commission. Some customers dislike salespeople who give them unsolicited assistance, particularly when they do so for the sole purpose of stopping other colleagues from doing it. Customers sometimes complain that they were given advice by a salesperson who did not know the product they were inquiring about, or that different salespeople give them different information about the same product. It must also be noted that the employees, even when they are with customers, watch one another constantly; so much so that it is not uncommon to see employees – when they find that a colleague is selling more than they are – walk away from an undecided customer so as to make a sale with another customer.

Reinforced rivalry

This is a good example of a system in which individuals get caught up in a mimetic spiral that generates envy, rivalry, and violence, used deliberately to stimulate individuals. The employees are forced to constantly compare themselves to one another and their self-esteem is under permanent attack. The feeling of inferiority triggered by the process of comparison associated with the designation of models (top, second, third) is exploited as a means of stimulating employees to increase their productivity. The object (making sales, earning more commissions, and/or win a contest) is nothing but a pretext for individuals who are obsessed about the others and about their respective positions.

Of course, the individuals in question do not perceive this object as secondary, as their income depends on it. It is even transfigured by the mimetic desire: the moment the others seem to desire it with the same intensity, it becomes essential. This process is evident during internal contests between the store's employees; external observers might consider that the prizes for these contests are insignificant in relation to the amount of energy invested to obtain them: a bottle of champagne, a CD, a discount voucher – anything will do as long as the subject believes it is desirable and desired by enough people. This is when the cycle of mimetic rivalry begins.

The generalization of envy is facilitated by the fact that the management has eliminated all boundaries and differences between the employees. As a result, the employees become more and more "alike" one another: whether they are employed under open-ended, fixed-term contracts, or are trainees, whether they work full or part time, the salespeople all compete under the same criterion (turnover). Whatever their specialization and initial qualifications, they are encouraged to sell all products offered by the store.

In an environment where differences are progressively eroded, individuals are trapped in a spiral that crushes them. With no boundaries to channel mimetic desire, people become more and more "alike" and the mimesis becomes increasingly virulent and widespread. Boundaries have been lifted, differences eliminated, and violence takes over. Each individual is ineluctably pushed further and further into a mimetic process and a spiral of envy and rivalry. The management team plays a fundamental role here as it intentionally reinforces the phenomenon:

- by systematizing a comparison process based on very few criteria (which reinforces the "likeness" between the employees);
- by making the comparison process explicit and by designating models;
- by combining comparison with judgments of value that play on the individuals' pride;
- by contributing to making the object (the targeted turnover; the bottle of champagne) desirable.

At what cost?

This system might seem to work for the organization, as indeed the overall performance of the store, and more generally of the group, is satisfactory, but this comes at a high cost: mediocre customer service, high staff turnover, an unpleasant working environment, and the employees' inability to work in teams. If more complex and subtle criteria (client satisfaction, customer loyalty, recruitment costs, etc.) were used to evaluate performance, the results obtained would be relatively lower. The exploitation of envy as a basis for a management policy has produced a degree of emulation but has also unleashed a spiral of violence, the consequences of which the management team has not tried to alleviate and which could, in time, have highly damaging consequences for the organization.

This extreme example has helped to reveal a number of organizational characteristics that are likely to generate envy among employees: when the system is based on a permanent comparison between individuals, and what is more makes this comparison explicit; when it causes people to interpret the gaps between individuals as differences in personal worth. Let us take a look at these practices.

Systems that promote comparison and the development of envy

The front cover of the October 2005 issue of a management magazine[7] well known in France says it all: it pictures an arm with big, blown-up biceps and a tape-measure around it. The title on the cover reads "How you are evaluated at work". The analogy is clear: what is evaluated is performance. Evaluation is reduced to a measurement; it is quantified and the measurement criterion is the same for everyone: the meter, the yardstick by which all individuals, whatever their function and the nature of their activities, are measured. Thus, each employee is reduced to one dimension and can therefore be compared to any other employee: employees measure themselves against the average for all employees. This representation is far from anecdotal. On the contrary, it seems to describe in a nutshell the practices of evaluation, comparison, and motivation that currently prevail in most organizations.

Hyper-rationalization, computerization, and increasing standardization

The more alike and comparable individuals become, the higher the probability that the mimetic process will be triggered and – as a result of the reciprocity phenomenon discussed in Chapter 3 – will lead to generalized envy and violence. Mimetic desire creates "sameness" and likeness, and eliminates personal identity. In traditional human societies, according to Girard, the fundamental function of all aspects of life is to constantly create differences so that individuals can be distinguished one from the other, and thus make it easier to limit the mimetic processes, while concealing the very existence of these processes. In some traditional societies, family resemblances between twins, for example, are feared because any resemblance is believed to lead to conflict and to a repetition of violence. Most rituals are unconsciously designed to reintroduce differences between members of the community, and the purpose of social rules is to maintain those differences. Thus, men look for a wife outside the family; age-related distinctions are clearly made through well-marked rites of passage.

In contemporary organizations, on the the other hand, management systems and practices tend to facilitate comparison between individuals.

An obsession for performance

In most firms, but also in public organizations, practices of evaluation, motivation, and of career management are based primarily on a restricted number of criteria and objectives. The never-ending quest for performance and the simple criteria used to measure it (sales or the profit margins realized) are now the rule rather than the exception. Organizations use standardized management and measurement tools to analyze and control the activities of most employees on the basis of a few indicators, which, in practice, boil down to quantitative volumes and values of the activity.

I discussed the case of Punchy earlier, but in all retail firms the most used performance indicators are the sales figures and margins realized, on a daily basis, by each department, each store, each region, etc.[8] In most retail groups, department managers are evaluated daily and compared, not only with the other department managers in their store, but also and above all with managers in charge of departments considered similar to theirs in other stores. The commercial departments of all enterprises, regardless of their sector of activity, have for a long time used those tools to determine goals for their sales force and to measure their activities. At McDonald's,[9] the productivity of the cashiers is evaluated hourly and measured on the basis of the amount of payments they have collected, whereas the kitchen staff's productivity is evaluated on the basis of their losses and of their ability to deliver the orders on time. An endless list of examples could be given as, indeed, most organizations use these types of methods.

Criteria of performance measurement have been used for a long time in most contemporary organizations – organizations that developed in the 20th century on the basis of Taylor's principles of rational management.

This rationalization has further intensified since, with groups such as McDonalds, which symbolize the hyper-rationalization of processes.[10] The now systematic use of computers and of Enterprise Resource Planning (ERP) systems, which integrate all data and processes of an organization into a unified system, has reinforced this evolution by enabling organizations to measure more and more precisely, and in real time, the activity of each individual, and to standardize and rationalize the management process.

Norms, standards, and labels

In addition to this is a widespread obsession, in all sectors of activity, with norms, standards, and labels.[11] Thus, the International Organization for Standardization (ISO) – the largest standardization organization in the world, whose main activity is the development of technical standards – now plays an essential role in most sectors.

The vast majority of ISO standards are highly specific to a particular product, material, or process. However, ISO 9000 and ISO 1400, used in organizations all over the world, are "generic management system standards". "Generic" means that the same standard can be applied to any organization, large or small, whatever its product or service, in any sector of activity, and whether it is a business enterprise, a public administration, or a government department. A "management system" is what an organization does to manage its processes and activities.[12]

This growing prevalence of norms and standards has resulted in an increasing use of common quantitative criteria that help evaluate the activity of the members of any organization and, thus, guarantee the quality of the processes implemented.

The tendencies I have just outlined apply to all sectors: organizations, regardless of their sector of activity, all strive to optimize their processes and are helped in their quest by the generalized use of computers and standardization procedures. The consequence of this tendency is that all activities are reduced to quantitative objectives and criteria according to which individuals are controlled, evaluated, and often motivated.[13]

The use of common criteria

What are the consequences of this phenomenon in terms of comparison between individuals? For comparison to be possible, there needs to be either common criteria or different criteria that can be brought to a common standard. Experts in decision-making call this "inter-criteria commensurability". For example, to decide on what car to buy, a potential buyer can find out whether the retail price of a car makes up for its average fuel consumption. This method requires that criteria such as price and consumption, which are a priori very different, be compatible or "commensurable".

The need to simplify

Making different criteria commensurable (or comparable) requires cognitive effort. So, what do we generally do when we need to compare different possibilities and when certain criteria only apply to some possibilities? We simplify! We use only the criteria that apply to all possibilities to simplify our calculations. In a well-known experiment on decision-making, a number of subjects were asked to compare pairs of students.[14] The students of each pair had scores on two dimensions: one common dimension (level of English proficiency) and a unique dimension (quantitative aptitude for one student and need to achieve success for the other). The subjects were asked to compare the students in each pair, so as to rank them. The results showed that the experimental subjects gave more weight to the common dimension (level of English), even though they had been cautioned against this tendency before the experiment. Other experiments have confirmed that individuals tend to use the criteria that are common to several options and to neglect those that are specific to each option.

Common, but simplistic, criteria

What does this imply with respect to individuals in organizations? How are they evaluated and compared? What are the criteria used to define and evaluate their activity? Quite logically, we observe that the criteria that are actually used are simplified. Those that are specific to one activity are generally neglected in favor of common criteria, which provide a simplified and quantifiable basis for comparison: i.e. those related to the individual contributions to the turnover, to the margin and profitability. This is what the tape-measure around the blown-up biceps pictured on the front cover of the magazine described above represents.

At McDonald's, for example, although specific criteria are used to evaluate each type of activity (tills, lobby, kitchen), the criteria that are given the most consideration are those related to turnover and productivity (the hourly turnover rate) – even when this has a negative impact on the qualitative aspects of the activity. At rush hour, for instance, McDonald's cashiers compete for the highest sales figures at the expense of the quality of the service they provide: because cashiers have to work fast, they have absolutely no time to develop any kind of relationship with the customers; interaction with customers is kept to a minimum and the latter are dealt with in an almost robotic manner; the cashier suggests certain products so as to shorten the customers' decision-making process (for example, cashiers systematically ask them if they would like Coke instead of asking them *what*, in the menu, they would like to order). If one of the products ordered is not ready immediately, the customer is made to wait while the cashier takes the next customer's order, and so on and so forth.[15]

The example of training and research in management

The increasing use of simple and quantitative criteria and as a result the lack of consideration given to the specific nature of each activity are not exclusive to the business world. In the field of research and training in management for example,[16] the evaluation model, first developed in the United States, is now used in all research organizations throughout the world, engaged in international competition. Researchers are evaluated on the basis of quantitative criteria, such as the number of publications and the ranking of the journals in which their articles are published.

The perverse effects of this system are well known: it encourages the race for publication, but in doing so forces researchers to sometimes publish the same studies – albeit with a few superficial alterations – in several journals or to break their articles up into several pieces, at the risk of compromising the integrity of the whole theoretical structure. In this system, the publication of books has far less value than the publication of articles, because the latter allow for a more standardized and therefore more quantifiable format.

In addition to this are the implications of the accreditation and certification schemes in which most universities and business schools are enrolled. An increasing number of educational organizations seek to have their training programs accredited by the AACSB (Association to Advance Collegiate Schools of Business, an association that certifies the "quality" of MBA programs) and/or by the EFMD (European Foundation for Management Development, a European organization that grants the EQUIS quality label to business schools). Certification implies a standardization and homogenization of the educational programs[17] that are accredited. For example, when the management education program offered by a management school is EQUIS certified, it means that the school has a large permanent faculty of high-quality teachers/researchers. But how are teachers/ researchers evaluated? By using the quantitative evaluation system described above. The different systems therefore reinforce one another and lead to a simplifying quantification of research and educational activities.

Producing sameness

Let us sum up the above considerations: what are the effects, in terms of envy, of systems that are increasingly based on inter-individual comparison – comparison facilitated by the growing use of standards and simplified and quantitative criteria? It is not our intention here to question the part played by such organizational and management systems in improving product and service quality and increasing the productivity of organizations that are governed by such systems. Our objective here is to examine the role that contemporary management systems play in the emergence and development of envy in the workplace.

Let us take another look at the mimetic theory: the more alike individuals are, the more differences disappear, and the higher the probability that the model will become the object of envy and a rival. And as it happens, contemporary management systems contribute to erasing differences between individuals, whose activities and performance are reduced to a few common criteria and indicators, regardless of their specificity. Thus, individuals become more alike and more comparable to one another, which makes envy a potential – but invisible and never acknowledged – consequence of these systems. The proximity or "alikeness" between individuals can be difficult to perceive for, in appearance, many things differentiate individuals: they are gauged on different levels and each individual is convinced that he/she is evaluated individually. But the bases for comparison are common to all and the attributes that are specific to each particular individual are ignored in favor of a few common dimensions. Individuals imitate one another on these common dimensions and soon there are no longer any subjects or models: there are people who become more and more alike and who do everything to deny this alikeness. The case of Punchy provides a perfect illustration of this process.

The fact that the short name chosen for the International Organization for Standardization – ISO – and for the standards it develops means "equal" is no accident: *because "International Organization for Standardization" would have different acronyms in different languages, [. . .] its founders decided to give it a name derived from the Greek isos, meaning "equal". Thus, the short form of the organization's name is always ISO.*[18] As for the European label "EQUIS", it is derived from the Latin *aequi*, which also means "equal". Behind these labels and standards – used more and more extensively in both private and public organizations in all sectors of activity – there is an intention: to produce "sameness", alikeness so as to facilitate comparison.

Interchangeable places

In addition to the factors I have just discussed, another aspect contributes to erasing differences within organizations and to facilitating the production of "sameness".

The question of place is fundamental in envy. The system of places usually refers to a system of differences. The more qualitative differences and nuances there are between individuals, the lower the probability that the mimetic process will be triggered and the less opportunity there is for envy to occur. But the evolution that has occurred in organizations has resulted in a break from the system in which all individuals had their respective places.

Indeed, since the 1990s, under the pressure exerted by management consultants and managerial trends, and in an attempt to reduce costs, organizations have tended to simplify their processes and to reduce the number of hierarchical levels (*downsizing*). Furthermore, there has been a tendency towards increasing flexibility in the places of individuals within organizations (a direct effect of *the reengineering craze* that swept the business world in the 1990s).

The effects and ravages of reengineering[19]

The Business Process Reengineering method, developed by Michael Hammer and James Champy, was popularized in the 1990s by consulting firms. It consisted of reorganizing enterprises by fundamentally reconsidering and redesigning organizational processes. The ultimate objective was to achieve productivity gains (of 30 to 60 percent). But although this target was, in most cases, never reached – partly because both the power of resistance to change and the hidden costs of any reorganization process were largely underestimated – the *business process reengineering* craze has had a profound and long-term impact on the way enterprises are run, by popularizing the idea that contemporary businesses should be able to rapidly and regularly reorganize their processes so as to adapt to their markets, technological changes, and evolutions in competing companies.

The concepts of staff flexibility and adaptability, which have become the leitmotiv of modern management, latently imply the erasure of differences. No one stays in the same place for very long and each individual is likely to take the place of another individual. Whereas the evolution of individuals used to be determined by the level of seniority and experience, and by the progressive completion of certain stages that were well defined and known in advance, the redesign and reorganization of systems and functions, which now seem to be undertaken on a regular basis, have blurred the functional boundaries that once separated individuals and have made the path of each person invisible. The less stability there is in the roles and functions of individuals in organizations, the more difficult it is for them to find a place or role they can refer to to define themselves, to define their own particular identity.

Here again, the Punchy example provides a good illustration of this phenomenon. The hierarchical structure of the store is very simple and flat: the management team consists of only two people. The already fragile boundaries separating the different departments disappear altogether when the management hires a saleswoman who seems to have the ability to sell any product from any department. The only thing that differentiated the employees, prior to the recruitment of the new saleswoman, was the fact that each of them was assigned to one specific department in priority (but not exclusively). This differentiation disappears the moment competition between the different salespeople takes place at store level and no longer at department level: each individual can take someone else's place and none have their own dedicated place. This phenomenon is also reflected in the daily sales contest, in which no one holds the same ranking position for very long. A salesperson may rank first one day and last the next day, and vice versa. The interchangeability of places puts all the employees on the same level, regardless of whether they are new or not, trainees or permanent employees, employed under open or fixed term contracts.

In order to understand how organizational systems can exploit envy, it therefore seems necessary to understand how, and on what basis, positions are attributed to individuals.

The "staging" of comparisons

The designation of models

Comparing individuals is not in itself enough to stimulate envy. Staging the comparison and designating models are essential.

As I have already mentioned, the etymology of the word "envy" is clear in this regard: envy is derived from the Latin *invidia*, which itself is derived from the verb *invidere*, meaning "to look askance at somebody" or "with a malicious eye". Envy is the "gaze disorder";[20] indeed, it is through the gaze that the envious becomes aware of an other, an other who seems to have what he/she is deprived of. In many societies, it is customary for people to hide that which they have more of than others – be it successfully harvested crops, good health, or good fortune, etc. – so as not to awaken envy in other people.[21] In some communities, people underplay what they possess for this purpose.

The importance of the gaze in the genesis of envy draws our attention to the impact of the explicit staging of comparisons in some organizations. Let us have a look at what takes place at Punchy. The management makes an outrageous show of the comparison: the results of all the salespeople are displayed daily, in the most exposed and therefore most visible area of the store; the names of not only the top three salespeople, but also of the one who scored the lowest, are clearly displayed; the frequent contests and associated prizes are a means of exposing those who do better than others to the gaze of everyone else.

In the case of the "Winning Factor" program, what triggers the emergence of envy in the organization is the ceremony (which is purposefully set up in such a way as to remind everyone of an Oscar award ceremony) in which some employees are presented, for all their colleagues to see, as heroes individually rewarded for excellent work.

Case 15: **The top employees go on vacation**[22]

In a chain of hair salons, the hairdressers who achieve the highest turnover rates win a trip to a holiday resort abroad.

In the salons in which one or more hairdressers are designated as the winners of the vacation, the work atmosphere generally deteriorates during the few weeks following the winner's vacation, and teamwork takes a back seat. These consequences are problematic because for a hairdressing business to run smoothly it is necessary for the hairdressers to be able to collaborate with one another. For example, the hairdressers must, depending on their availability, be willing to answer the phone and greet customers. Although they each have their own customers to take care of, they must also pay attention to their colleagues' customers; they must all be willing to replace a towel that has dropped on the floor, or place magazines on the various tables and worktops, tell a colleague that a timer he/she set has gone off, offer a cup of coffee to someone else's customer, etc. The hairdressers also have to help each other when one is running late and another is ahead of schedule, or when a customer is in a hurry; thus, it is not uncommon for hairdressers to wash or dry the hair of one of their colleagues' customers. This type of help is provided informally, and depends on the availability of each hairdresser, and on his/her presence in such or such an area of the salon.

The deterioration of the atmosphere and of teamwork takes the form of a decrease in service quality and of a feeling of dissatisfaction with work. A close examination of the situation reveals that the problems are partly rooted in envy: the hairdressers who stay behind envy those who went away on vacation, all the more so as they are forced to attend to their colleagues' customers in their absence, and explain to them why their hairdresser is not at work. This makes them feel as if the performance differences are staged and exposed not only internally but also externally since they are forced to tell the customers why their colleagues are absent: as far as the envious are concerned, the implicit message to the customer is "we've stayed behind because we are not as good as the others". When the winners come back from their vacation, the fact that they have a nice tan and look relaxed further contributes to showing that they have been rewarded.

In these three cases, no one avoids comparison; the employees cannot but be aware of their position in relation to the others and cannot but fix their gaze on those who have been designated as the best by the system. There is no escape and the others always become models (and implicitly, rivals since they represent what has to be achieved). The others are those who achieve and are rewarded for their achievements; what makes them enviable is their success and the rewards they get for it (sometimes money, a promotion, or a trip, but in most cases the reward is symbolic in that it lies in the fact that it is staged for all to see).

My hypothesis therefore is that organizations that stage comparisons – by displaying the results of each employee for all to see, and by designating the "best" employees and rewarding them symbolically and/or concretely for their achievements – are more likely than others to produce envy and therefore to suffer its effects.

Forced ranking

One evaluation method – the "forced ranking" system, currently in wide use in many enterprises – most probably contributes to the development of envy and to its potentially dangerous consequences. This system was established years ago at companies like General Electric. Since then, many enterprises (for example, 3M, Boeing, Honeywell, Home Depot) have adopted this method of evaluation, in which employees are ranked against each other along a bell-shaped distribution curve. It identifies, for instance, the top 20 percent, who are rewarded accordingly, the middle 70 percent, for whom development objectives are set, and finally the bottom 10 percent, who are either closely monitored or forced to resign. The main characteristic of this method is that all individuals are compared to one another, rather than to themselves (i.e. past performance or their performance at another post) or to specific objectives related to their own post. Here again this evaluation method necessitates common criteria for all types of activity, and the comparison with others cannot be avoided.

Under serious criticism

Though these evaluation systems have been widely used in large firms and advocated by many consultants, they have nonetheless come under serious, and well-documented, criticism. Such practices have negative consequences in certain types of environment, particularly in organizations where teamwork is essential.[23] In a survey of 200 human resources management professionals working in firms of over 2500 employees,[24] more than half of which used a forced ranking system, the respondents emphasized the negative effects of these practices: low productivity, less collaboration, feelings of unfairness, skepticism and even disengagement on the part of the workforce, mistrust towards the management team.

In these systems, a small proportion of the individuals is highly praised and explicitly distinguished from the others. The gaps between the worst and best-paid employees are very wide. A survey conducted in American universities has shown that the lecturers who were the least satisfied were those who worked in departments in which income inequalities were larger, even when those inequalities were related to factors such as research productivity or experience.[25]

An impact on quality or performance

A study based on a sample of 102 business units belonging to 41 corporations in America and England demonstrated that the higher the pay differentials between the top executives and the other employees – particularly the lowest paid ones – the more the quality of what the business unit produces decreases.[26] It is clear here that the system has negative effects not only on the satisfaction and morale of the employees or on their involvement, but also on the quality of the products or services provided. According to the authors of the study, the employees perceive the wide gaps between the lowest and highest paid individuals as unfair; this decreases their motivation to achieve the goals set by the firm, and their willingness to cooperate, which in turn impacts on the quality of what they produce. Another survey of several hundred corporations has shown that managerial turnover was higher, and average tenure lower, in organizations that had more dispersion in their pay structures.[27]

A similar phenomenon can be observed in the sports world, where teamwork and collaboration are particularly important. In one instance, a study of 1500 baseball players in 29 different teams over an eight-year period showed that the teams in which the pay differentials between the players were the highest were also the teams that won the fewest games and had low advertising revenues.[28]

Thus, it has been demonstrated that systematically comparing individuals (by putting them on a common scale, their position on which seems to be the only thing which, as far as the system is concerned, differentiates them from one another) and presenting a few individuals as heroes, has perverse consequences. This supports our hypothesis: this type of system contributes to the development of envy which manifests itself through symptoms such as discontent, job dissatisfaction, poor working atmosphere, and decreased performance.

A system that impacts on self-esteem

Interpreting differences between individuals as differences in worth

As mentioned in Chapter 1 with respect to the comparison process and envy, it is not the comparison itself that engenders envy in the subjects, but the conclusions the envious draw from it in terms of their self-representation and self-worth. Interpreting the success of another person as a personal loss or failure, or as a sign of inferiority, predisposes the subject to become envious. The question to be raised here is therefore: *what in organizational and management systems leads individuals to make such interpretations?*

How traditional societies protect themselves from envy

Anthropologists have shown that many traditional social systems[29] allow people who temporarily find themselves in a situation of inferiority to attribute their misfortune to external forces over which they have no power. Their personal qualities are therefore not called into question, nor do they have to acknowledge their own limitations, and as a result they have no reason to envy their more fortunate neighbors. In the traditional farming communities of Mexico for example, it would be quite normal for people to say about a member of the community whose circumstances have improved: "This farmer has more than we do, but that's because he has discovered a hidden treasure or he has won the lottery; so why should we envy him?" The possibility of attributing the success of others to fate, coincidence, luck, or to forces that cannot be controlled enables the members of these communities to protect the psychological balance of those who find themselves in a situation of inferiority – and who might believe that fate will one day be kind to them – and to prevent the arousal of envy.[30]

Nothing happens by accident

It is obvious that there is no place for this type of interpretation system in contemporary organizations. On the contrary, the culture of results and the factors of evolution described earlier privilege the measurement of results and the attribution of the latter to personal causes. Thus, in the "Winning Factor" program, and in the case of Punchy and of most organizations, individuals are evaluated and motivated on the basis of their results; results considered to be the direct consequences of their actions and, implicitly, of their capacities. The tendency to overestimate the role of internal characteristics (the abilities and personality of an individual) and to underestimate that of external factors (related to circumstances) to explain the behavior or results of others is known to social psychologists as the "Fundamental Attribution Error". Comparative cultural studies have shown that this tendency is far more prevalent in western cultures than in others.[31]

At Punchy, experience, the training opportunities offered by the management to some employees, or the coincidence by which customers approach one salesperson rather than another are not considered factors that impact on results. All individuals are comparable with one another and the sales results achieved by each employee are interpreted according to a simple rule of cause and effect: the salespeople who achieve good results are good, those who get average results are average, and those who get bad results are bad. The director's written comments accompanying the daily score of each employee are crystal clear in their meaning.

In this context, the performance appraisal system is a source of threat: over the salespeople there hangs a constant sense of threat, and of uncertainty about what will happen to them and about their own worth, which fosters envy.[32]

Simplified cause and effect links

The vast majority of people adapt their behavior to the management tools that measure and evaluate their activity: they choose actions that can have an impact on what is measured and avoid those whose effects are less visible and unmeasured.[33] I gave the example earlier of McDonald's cashiers who, because they are evaluated mainly on the basis of their hourly sales results, choose during rush hour to neglect service quality and focus on speed and productivity. Out of all the goals they could pursue, they concentrate on those that significantly influence the evaluation of their activity, even if in doing so their behavior impacts negatively on other aspects.

All these processes show that the results organizations take into consideration are generally interpreted as a direct consequence of a person's actions, an interpretation that tends to encourage certain types of behavior that are supposed to have certain consequences

("You've got to taunt their pride and push them to react" says Punchy's director). In this type of system, it is difficult to attribute the results to causes other than the behavior of individuals. Yet, in most cases, the results depend on a combination of factors, such as the actions of competing companies (or the absence of competitors), the market situation, factors related to each person's experience, coincidence, rebound effects, etc. If and when these other factors are taken into account, it is difficult to determine their respective impact. It is much easier, and more in line with the western ideology of mastery and control, to attribute the causes of a result to the will and actions of such and such a person!

A direct consequence of this interpretation system is that it becomes difficult not to believe that "the other has more than I do because he/she is better than I am. I alone am the cause of this difference". As explained in Chapter 1, interpretations of this type foster envy. We touch here on an active, yet never considered, consequence of the management systems that are now in use in most organizations.

The rise of frustration and the inescapable grip of envy

Envy is often related to frustration: the other has something that I do not have. However, in many cases this feeling does not last, either because individuals obtain what they desire or because they renounce it and turn towards models that are easier to imitate. What is fundamental in this process is that individuals normally manage to steer their attention away from the idea that what other possess they must acquire too. In the worst cases of envy, however, the envious remain fixated on this idea and can end up spending large amounts of psychological energy desiring what they can never possess. Frustration can then take on enormous proportions.

Can envy serve as a stimulus?

To understand how organizational systems foster envy, and above all how they sometimes cause envy to do serious damage, it is necessary to examine what in these systems is likely to generate and maintain frustration among individuals. We believe that organizations that allow frustration to fester are also those in which envy can reach dangerous proportions. The problem arises when nothing in the system enables its members to escape envy, or to use it as a stimulus to progress. In short, when individuals get stuck in an impasse, they cannot but desire what the system designates as the unique object of desire (via those who are successful), but they never seem to reach it.

In the Hong Kong bank, however, envy does occur among the employees who have not been promoted, but it does not reach dangerous proportions: those who felt envious of their colleagues are also those who achieved the best performance results a few months after their application for promotion was rejected. In this case, envy has served as a stimulus and has not turned into aggression. For most, the fact that promotion reviews are conducted on a regular basis and that a relatively large proportion of employees are granted promotion probably reassures them that their time will come. They perceive their failure as temporary, and so can motivate themselves to improve their performance so that they have a better chance of being promoted next time. The feeling of inferiority only lasts for a moment and the organizational context allows for a conversion of envy (or for its disappearance?) into a motivation to improve.

The "one best way" impasse

Not all organizational systems allow for such evolutions. Some systems can, for example, give their members the impression that the only path to career development is the *royal path*; the latter simultaneously becomes the only truly valued (and therefore desirable) path, reserved for a very small number of rival pretenders competing with one another in accordance with certain rigid rules. In some bureaucracies, for example, the possibilities of career advancement are governed by strict and restrictive rules, making the paths to progress very rigid and greatly reducing people's chances of advancing in their careers.

In cases like these, deviating from the *royal path* will be interpreted as a lack of competence rather than a choice made by the person. In environments where individuals who do not "climb up the career ladder" are judged as lacking the attributes required to do so, envy is likely to develop. Simultaneously, the fact that other career paths are not valued by the organization prevents individuals from focusing their attention on models that might suit them better and be accessible. In such situations, frustration rises and with it envy comes to a head and is likely to take the form of aggressive behavior towards either the system or the people who succeed. Another scenario is that the feeling of inferiority the system has fostered can cause individuals to lose trust in their own abilities, and this can result in long-term demotivation, a disengagement from the system, and/or depressive behavior (a behavioral consequence of envy discussed in Chapter 2).

I cannot emphasize enough the noxiousness, in terms of envy, of systems that consider only one type of path as valuable, do not respect other possible alternative routes that one could choose in relation to one's profession, and at the same time make the "one best way" almost inaccessible to most people. Systems like these cannot but systematically foster envy. An example is given at the end of the chapter.

The role of the manager

All the factors discussed above can contribute to the systematic development of envy within the organizations in which they exist. Let us now look at one last factor, which I consider to be essential and likely to have an impact on all the others: the role played by the management team. In Chapter 2, I gave the example of a study showing that there is a link between the feelings of envy that team workers can experience and the poor relationship they have with their direct supervisor.[34] The study highlights this link without explaining it. Does being envious lead to a general resentment against the system as a whole, and therefore against one's supervisor as a representative of this system? Or does the fact that employees do not get on with their boss cause them to believe that the latter favors some team members over them and therefore contributes to the development of envy?

A priori, neither hypothesis can be rejected. But I wish to discuss another one. Within a team, the manager plays a fundamental role: the functioning rules and management methods are applied, in practice, via the manager. The manager is therefore in a position to make the factors described above more or less prevalent within a team, and therefore to let them contribute more or less to the development of envy.

In this respect the Punchy case is very interesting: the director plays a central role in the generalized spreading of envy in his store. He systematizes the permanent comparison between individuals, using a very small number of criteria, and in doing so reinforces the practices advocated by the head office. He promotes the development of mimetic behavior by encouraging the salespeople to work in all the sections of the store, regardless of the section to which they have been appointed. He patently stages the comparison by displaying the daily scores of all the employees and systematically referring to the "best salespeople" during his interviews with his employees. He makes sure that the differences between the salespeople are interpreted as differences in worth by adding comments to the daily results of each person. Finally, by refusing to intervene in the daily conflicts between the salespeople, he causes envy to have serious consequences for the system.

Limitless envy: a production of the system

The Punchy case has helped us see in what way the different factors discussed in this chapter could promote the systematic development of envy in an organization. This example is emblematic of what takes place in many organizations in which the never-ending quest for greater productivity rests on competition and rivalry, and as a result generates envy. Let us now describe another case of envy that takes place in an organization that differs vastly from the Punchy organization, and which will help us gain a clearer picture of the processes described in this chapter.

Case 16: **The business school case**
Mr Choum is the director of a business school[35] that is already well positioned among similar schools in France. For a few years, he has been seeking to strengthen the school's position both nationally and internationally. All reputable schools and universities are well endowed with professors who are highly involved in research.

To achieve the development goals he has set out for the school, Mr Choum considers that his priority is to further develop research activities, which leads him to recruit academics with doctorates and who have already published articles, preferably in English. As the school does not have the means nor, yet, the reputation to attract confirmed researchers, the new recruits are young (aged between 26 and 33). To help position the school as a quality school, Mr Choum also decides to apply for the EQUIS accreditation we mentioned above, which leads him to place the researchers in a foreground position.

Within two years, researchers are catapulted into the highly valued category of lecturers. And yet they are not the only representatives of the teaching faculty. Indeed, the school has for many years employed teachers who also have experience in the business world and who, for the most part, worked as instructors or as developers/facilitators of training programs. These teachers are much older (approximately 50 years of age) and less highly qualified than the researchers, but have more experience in program management and have more contacts in the business world.

At the time the academics with "research" profiles were recruited, the heads of department (marketing, finance, strategy, etc.) were all "senior lecturers". As soon as enough young teachers were recruited (after about two years), Mr Choum decided to give them most of the posts of responsibility in the school, in particular those of heads of departments and of cross-department management (academic management, cultural development management, responsibilities related to the accreditation process, etc). In addition to transferring responsibilities from the "seniors" to the "new recruits", Mr Choum made them change offices: those among the "seniors" who previously held posts of responsibility had to move from the fifth storey (the management storey) to the third storey, while the "new recruits" who had progressively been given offices on the third storey were moved to the fifth storey.

In order to clearly show off those among the teachers who have a "research" profile, a short resume is displayed on their doors providing information concerning the person's responsibilities in the organization, his/her diplomas (Grande Ecole, doctorate), fields of research and education. The other teachers are subsequently also required to display their resume on their doors, which of course makes the differences between the teachers plainly visible. As far as resource allocation is concerned, the priority given to research activities implies that all necessary resources are made available to those who need to attend conferences. On the other hand, the resources allocated to the "others", particularly those needed to be able to travel, are reduced.

The "new recruits" are regularly put in the spotlight during events or functions that symbolically highlight the position of each lecturer, either within the management circle (i.e. a valued position) or outside it (i.e. a position with no value). These events include official receptions in prestigious restaurants with members of other organizations or businesses, residential seminars on the school's educational strategy, and a seminar held at the beginning of each school year attended by all members of the school. Many talk of the "seraglio" in reference to the management circle.

This whole system causes a lot of tension between the members of the faculty: the "seniors" become demotivated and complain constantly, while most of the "new" teachers feel uncomfortable about the excessive praise and emphasis given to their specific qualifications, and feel that they have usurped the place of the "seniors", in particular by taking over their offices. Envy reigns within the school and manifests itself through offensive remarks against the new recruits or through a difficulty to work in teams. Many end up handing in their resignation, particularly among the new recruits, who find it difficult to operate in such a conflictual environment. The high turnover rate runs counter to the school's development strategy. This soaring turnover rate is all the more worrying as the production of PhD graduates is limited, and schools and universities therefore have to compete to attract them. Finally, the director of the school is often said to "divide and rule", which seems a fair comment since he does indeed divide the members of the faculty by generating envy among the teachers who do not have a research profile.

All the factors discussed in this chapter are present in the school's management system:

- The latter is based on permanent comparison: the teachers are compared and ranked according to a small set of criteria supposed to determine the value of each one;
- This comparison is staged in so far as each teacher's "performance" – evaluated according to the criteria mentioned above – is displayed on his or her office door;
- These criteria (related to research) do not take into account the specificities of some categories of lecturers and their potential contributions to the development of the school: apart from the

"one best way" retained by the director, no other path or profile is valued, which causes a high level of frustration among the senior lecturers. In this system, a certain profile is designated as a model for all the members of the organization to follow;

- Places seem to be interchangeable: those who in the past were highly valued are now under-appreciated; the office moves symbolize this interchangeability. As a result, the places of individuals are not longer protected since all frontiers between them are blurred.

- The system's representative – i.e. the director – justifies these changes by saying, "those who are promoted to higher positions are promoted because they have value; those who are downgraded are downgraded because they have none". The system therefore interprets the gaps between the different lecturers as being directly related to an intrinsic quality. As a result, those who do not possess this quality feel inferior.

- The director, who makes all the decisions, plays a central role in the development of such a system.

Systems that induce envy

By permanently and systematically evaluating employees and their performance on the basis of a handful of selected criteria, and by blatantly comparing employees with one another, contemporary organizations can easily turn into breeding grounds for envy. It is not the occurrence of envy by itself that is problematic, as indeed envy is a fundamentally human emotion likely to arise among human beings living in groups. However, unlike traditional societies, which are organized in such a way as to limit and contain the potentially destructive effects of envy – by ensuring that the differences between individuals are maintained – contemporary organizations are based on management systems that reinforce the destructive effects of envy by promoting systematic comparison and mimetic processes. Because envy is never recognized for what it is in organizations – for the reasons discussed in Chapter 1 and in particular because it is socially unacceptable – it hides behind other dysfunctional symptoms such as violence between team members, intense rivalry, frenzied individualism, or a bad working atmosphere.

Card 3   Identifying the risks in my organization

Some management practices are more propitious than others to the systematic development of envy. Learn how to spot them. The more affirmative your answers to the statements given below are, the more active envy is likely to be in your organization.

Evaluation of performance

In practice, everything is reduced to a few criteria (for example, turnover and margin).

All individuals are evaluated according to the same criteria.

The measurement of performance is above all quantitative.

The measurement of performance is above all individual.

Performance is almost permanently evaluated (daily or weekly).

Everybody competes with everybody.

The results of every individual are always on display: individuals always know in what position they are in relation to others.

In the evaluation of individuals' performances, external factors (positive or negative) are never taken into account.

The performance frontiers keep on moving.

Retribution

Rewards are mostly individual.

We are regularly requested to attend ceremonies during which prizes are awarded: they are like "Oscar Award" ceremonies.

Employees are clearly categorized: there are the best performers, the average performers, and finally those who are really bad.

Possible advancement within the organization

The hierarchical structure is flat; there are few hierarchical levels.

It is very difficult to move from one level to another.

Possibilities to climb up the ladder are limited.

Apart from the *"one best way"*, nothing much is valued.

There is a vast difference between the "official" and the real career advancement rules.

5
Envy and Narcissism in Contemporary Organizations

The mimesis theory has the merit of drawing our attention to behaviors that are easily observed in human communities, whatever their nature, and of helping us find the link between mimetism, envy, and violence. One essential aspect of this theory is that it places emphasis on the fundamental role of the *other* in the problematic of envy; an *other* who initially serves as a model and who progressively turns into a rival as he/she draws the attention of the envious. Extrapolating from this theory, one could conclude that envy would not exist if the construction of the subject were not intrinsically related to the *other*. Yet, Girard's theory teaches nothing concerning this aspect. Based on the observation of mimetic behaviors, the theory merely reveals the fundamental role played by the *other* when he/she is used as a model, and states its consequences from an anthropological perspective. But it says nothing about the origin of this primordial "clash" with the other. Why does the other fascinate us so much? Why is the other placed in a position of model? Why does becoming like the model turn into a matter of life or death? Why are the slightest differences blown out of proportion by the person who "falls" victim to envy?

Psychoanalysis is the discipline that can best help us to answer these questions. By proposing a model of the psychological development of individuals, psychoanalysis takes us back to the infantile roots of envy and helps us understand what conditions the subject's relation to the *other*. This aspect matters not only because it helps us understand what envy is and where it comes from, but also helps us find out what, in the management practices of contemporary organizations, is more or less likely to reinforce the effects of envy. More precisely, psycho-analysis leads us to examine the *angle from which the figure of the "other" is presented and even used in organizations;* this will lead us to the question of narcissism in the workplace. My aim here is to examine more closely some aspects discussed in Chapter 4, in which I showed that putting models "on display" played a fundamental role in the genesis of envy in organizations.

Psychoanalytic contributions to understanding envy

One fundamental hypothesis of psychoanalysis is that envy is an infantile residue of the process of psychological development of all human beings and that its manifestation during adult life (in the workplace for example) is rooted in archaic processes; that is, in processes that took place in our earliest childhood.

Before going any further on this topic, we need to discuss the complex process through which we develop psychologically; a process during which the *other* plays an essential role.

Captured in an image

At birth and during the first months of their lives, children can neither talk nor walk. They do not yet have full control of their motor functions, and their biological development is not completed. They fantasmatically experience themselves as a body in pieces. A critical moment occurs in their development[1] when, looking at their own reflection in a mirror, they identify with an image outside themselves. Initially, it seems the children perceive the image they see in the mirror as that of a real being they try to approach. This first experience shows confusion between the self and the other.

In a second stage, children discover that the other in the mirror is not a real being but an image. Finally, they realize that the image in the mirror is their own; they recognize themselves through it, and in so doing can put together the pieces of the body to form an entity that is a representation of their body. The image of their body is therefore structuring for the subjects' identity, which develops as an entity thanks to external and symmetrically inverted (in the mirror) clues. In this process, they are fantasmatically "captured" by an image.

Many psychoanalysts consider this precise moment as the foundation of the construction of the "self" (*ego*) in the identity of a person: the self forms around this image of the body. However, this image is, first of all, inversed and therefore inauthentic, and secondly it conceals the incomplete and fragmented state of the body. The French psychoanalyst Lacan called the register in which this construction of the self takes place the "Imaginary", emphasizing the importance of the gaze and of the image in this process.

What is also fundamental about this stage, during which the ego is constructed, is that in order to identify himself with the image in the mirror, the child needs the presence of the adult next to him; he needs to find in the adult's gaze the confirmation that it is indeed himself that he is seeing in the mirror. The child only recognizes himself in his own image if he feels that the other (the mother) already identifies him as such.[2] He can only recognize himself if the other has recognized him first. The ego is therefore subjected to the other in two ways: firstly, it develops from the image that is first perceived as a real other before being identified as an image, and then as the image of the self; and secondly, this identification depends on the gaze of the other who gives him the confirmation that the image he sees is indeed his own.[3]

To differentiate these two "others", Lacan calls the other in the mirror the "little other", or simply "the other", and he calls the one who stands by the child and supports him, the one the child needs to recognize himself, "the big Other" or "the Other". I shall often refer to this useful distinction in the rest of this book.

The Oedipus complex and how the subject experiences lack and desire

Towards the end of the identification stage of the mirror phase, the child has formed a sense of self but does not yet feel like a separate being from his/her mother.

First phase: the exclusive object of the mother's desire

In what some consider as the first phase of the Oedipus complex,[4] children adopt a particular position vis-a-vis their mother by trying to identify with what they assume is the object of the latter's desire. They feel they are the exclusive object of their mother's desire, the only being capable of satisfying her entirely; that is, in more psychoanalytical terms, the object that fills the lack in the Other (the mother). In psychoanalysis, the object that is supposed to fill the lack in the Other is called the *phallus*.

Second phase: the mother's desire is directed towards the father

However, there comes a time when children are able to associate the absence of the mother with the presence of the father, and this triggers the second phase of the Oedipus complex. The children then perceive their father as the being towards whom their mother's desire is directed. They discover that their mother's desire is dependent on an object that the father is supposed to have. Furthermore, the father being the one who possesses the *phallus*, the latter becomes the object promised to the children for use in the future. This promise implies that what will be returned to the children in the future was first taken away. Thus, growing up supposes the acceptance of an initial loss.[5]

Third phase: introduction to lack and desire

This moment is fundamental for children, for they simultaneously lose the unified world in which they reigned and enter a world ruled by desire. The deficiencies they experience as a result of not entirely satisfying their mother, and of not possessing the *phallus* for the time being, show them that there is something other than unity: there is a world that is governed by desire. It is at that moment that the split from the mother can take place and that she becomes a truly distinct entity. It is also then that the children, now separate from their mother, are introduced to the existence of a law that is external to themselves, that precedes them and in relation to which they position themselves, within a system of differences. In Lacanian terms, this process, during which the initial wholeness of the world must be abandoned in order to reach a wider horizon and a world ruled by desire and law, gives access to what Lacan calls the "Symbolic realm", or more simply the "Symbolic".[6] This Symbolic realm refers to the social, cultural, and linguistic environment into which the children were born and which conditions their development.

Becoming a subject

From a narcissistic point of view, this moment is essential. Children become aware, through the presence of an other (the father), that they are no longer their mother's exclusive objects. This is the moment when the children become conscious of what the object of desire is and can stop identifying themselves with this object, thus partly freeing themselves from the illusion, from the image in which they had been trapped. They can position themselves as subjects and no longer as the Other's object of desire. It is under this condition that the children can start exploring the world around them. The beginning of desire (theirs) is a condition for the children to develop and grow. This stage introduces the subjects to the sense of loss inherent to any desire.

What is fundamental in this theory is that it highlights the fact that:

- The subjects initially develop through *identifications* (in particular, identification to the other in the mirror) in which the Other (with a capital A because he/she is the adult who validates these identifications) plays a fundamental role; it enables children to construct themselves as separate entities, which is the foundation of their identity.
- This process leads them also to be trapped in an image fundamentally alien to them, outside them. Firstly, indeed, they found their identity on an image of themselves that is automatically false (a reversed image, concealing a disturbing lack of unity). Secondly, the child is dependent on the Other to confirm his/her identity. This initial identification process lays the foundations of future identifications, where: (a) those who serve as models will be the other in the mirror; and (b) everything that validates the relevance of these identifications will have the role of the Other.
- By experiencing the Oedipus complex, children are progressively introduced to the register of the Symbolic, which requires the acceptance of lack and of the law. The symbolic dimension takes root in the psychic structure of individuals and prevents the latter from remaining trapped in the Imaginary Register in which they had built their initial identity.

Thus, individuals' psychological growth is based on two rather contradictory dimensions. On the one hand, children live under the illusion of being complete (role played by the "ego", an imaginary formation comforting the narcissistic experience of unity and continuity). And on the other, they are animated by a desire – the meaning of which they do not understand – related to an initial lack.

Envy in the construction of the self

What happens with envious subjects?[7] Instead of being driven by their own desires, envious subjects remain obsessed with desires that are mediated through the other; that is, the person they envy. Envious subjects cannot bear the lack they experience; and yet it is only through lack that individuals can become aware of their own separate identity and, therefore, that self-comparison with others ceases to be problematic. Envy is believed to be a consequence of the individuals' initial difficulty in freeing themselves from the original illusion that they were the Other's (the mother's) exclusive objects of desire. For envious individuals, there can only be one place: that of the individual on whom their mother – the Other – gazes. If this place is taken, there is no other possible place for them. Having lost their mother's gaze and therefore the image of themselves as complete and omnipotent coming from the Other's returning gaze, they are confronted with a void and with the feeling of no longer existing. They feel *"transparent"*.[8]

The feeling of no longer existing experienced by envious individuals is radical and is accompanied with immense narcissistic suffering. Because the envious remain confined in the Imaginary Register, their choice of object is then narcissistic: the person they envy is an other who is almost identical to themselves, one the envious perceive as possessing a precious object which they themselves do not have and which, they feel, is essential to their existence.

Envious individuals are very dependent on a representation of themselves and of the other as *complete* entities – a representation they inherited from the mirror phase.[9] The idea is that the *others* are not driven by lack, that they are complete and that they possess the key to what the envious cannot find in themselves. It is the trait the envied possess, and which the envious do not, that makes all the difference. And it is this "extra trait" that the envious will either seek to destroy, or try to appropriate for themselves.

Envious subjects remain prisoners of an imaginary triangle comprising themselves, the other (the "little other" in the sense meant by Lacan) fantasmatically perceived as complete, and the Other (the mother initially, and then everything which, through a transference process, takes her place) by whom the subjects need to be recognized, and whose desires the subjects feel they must satisfy. But the envious feel incapable of satisfying the Other's needs because the other already possesses what is needed to attract the Other's gaze.

Here lies the main difference between envy and jealousy. Envy originates in the pre-Oedipal phase of our psychological development; it is fundamentally related to our narcissism. Jealousy, a more "mature" emotion than envy, originates in the Oedipal phase of our development, a phase during which the child must learn to renounce the parent of the opposite sex as an object of sexual love. Jealousy implies that the subject feels separated and different from the person he/she is jealous of. It implies a true loss as opposed to a fantasmatic deficiency. Finally, jealousy is closely related to the moment when the subject's sexual identity is established, whereas envy originates in the moment when the subject's ego develops as a unified entity.

The psychological roots of mimetism

Envy can therefore be considered as corresponding, in subjects, to the pre-eminence of the Imaginary Register, on which they initially constructed themselves. This does not contradict the ideas described in Chapter 3 but rather helps us look at them from a different perspective.

In the psychoanalytical approach, mimetism is thought to be the residue of the development process of each human being, a process that necessarily includes a decisive passage through the other. The roots of imitation of and fixation to an other who is first model and then rival are to be found in this structural phase of our development. The emergence of envy in adult life unveils the "missed" stages of this development.

The two approaches (psychoanalysis and the mimetic theory) are complementary in helping us to understand envy in a social context: one helps us to understand the origin of envy, which is intrinsically related to the child's dependence on his/her mother and to the process during which the subject's ego is established; while the other helps identify and analyze the mechanism that produces envy in social relations, without examining the origins of this emotion.

According to René Girard, one of the most important roles of a social system is to prevent mimetic processes and the resulting envy and violence by maintaining the differences that separate the members of the system. In the psychoanalytical approach, it is the Symbolic that plays a central role: it introduces the subject to differences and prohibitions, and enables the child to distinguish him/herself from his/her image. The Symbolic serves as a mediator in the child's relation with reality, and prevents him/her from getting entirely caught up in his/her image or double.

Organization and the Imaginary Register

If the emergence of envy is related to the Imaginary, and in particular to its prevalence in a subject's psyche, a question of great importance to our understanding of envy in the workplace is whether contemporary organizations, through the management methods they implement, foster the prevalence of the Imaginary.

The answer to this question has already been given by a number of researchers[10] interested in the functioning of modern enterprises, or, as some call them, "hypermodern" organizations. However, the problematic of envy associated with this question has not yet been examined. I shall try and extend their analysis of organizations to explain the occurrence of envy.

From controlling the body to controlling the mind

These reflections are based, originally, on studies of large firms – American for the most part – such as IBM, Hewlett Packard, Procter&Gamble, American Express, and McDonald's. They also apply to many organizations of other nationalities; indeed, globalization of the economy, ever-increasing competition between firms and countries, the pressure from consulting firms, and even the success of a few management manuals have all contributed to the diffusion of similar management techniques. Most of these authors draw attention to one fundamental characteristic of these organizations: they gain a psychological hold over their employees by "trapping the latter in their own desires of narcissistic assertion and identification, in their fantasies of omnipotence or in their need for love".[11] In modern organizations – based on the Taylorian model – the primary objective was to increase efficiency by controlling the physical bodies of employees (via a strict control of their gestures); but in the organizations that these authors qualify as "hypermodern", the control is above all psychological.

Hypermodernity, understood as an exacerbation of modernity, is mostly characterized by sophisticated managerial techniques that enable organizations to gain the above-mentioned psychological hold over their employees by using what we have called the Imaginary Register. Some authors have coined the word "managinary" – merging the terms "management" and "imaginary" – to qualify such management systems.

A constant exploitation of individuals' narcissism

The Imaginary is mobilized, in part, by exploiting people's narcissism.

Contemporary organizations place individuals at the heart of the narcissistic question. The functions individuals must perform, their responsibilities, the projects they must undertake, and the objectives to be reached are all elements through which employees develop their identity. These functions play the role of a protective sheath by giving the employees a feeling of permanence and unity, and by reflecting a positive image of themselves.

Employees are constantly encouraged to identify themselves with the image of omnipotence and perfection conveyed by the organization. Challenges are not only welcome but also encouraged as employees attempt to constantly push their own limits and reach excellence. Surpassing oneself is not just desirable; it is presented as a way of discovering "who we are". Objective-based management enables the organization to push the limits further and further in an endless quest that projects an image of omnipotence onto the individual.

The theme of competition is omnipresent: global competition, competition with other enterprises – which use exactly the same management practices – or internal competition, between departments or between individuals, evaluated on the basis of common criteria. Mobilization must be constant for organizations to conquer market shares, beat their competitors, reduce costs, increase productivity, and grow. Success and victory are themes that are imprinted onto the minds of all members of organizations.

The system brings the employees face to face with an image of excellence, performance, richness, perfection, and youth. Through the systems of selection (the long and phased recruitment processes give the impression that the selection is strict), of incentives (objective-based management, bonuses determined according to

employees' performance and results), of evaluation (individualiza-
tion of performances, permanent feedback, reference to models,
comparison to others), or of career management (promotion/
individualized selection, competition between employees), people
are under constant pressure, and as a result become heavily engaged
in their work. There is a "narcissistic contract", so to speak, between
the organization and the employees: the latter "invest their narcissistic libido in a system they become part of and which offers them
recognition and idealization".[12]

A "Managinary" system and envy

The human costs associated with such practices are far from negligible. The over-importance placed on action, the obligation to be
strong, the obsession with winning, and the never-ending demand
for adaptability result in pathologies: because the individuals are
under constant pressure, they are at risk of professional exhaustion.
Captivated by the image of themselves conveyed to them by their
organization, they exert themselves for the good of the latter, but
might be overcome by a feeling of void: they are "drained", and are
left with no energy. When they can no longer meet the demand and
fulfill the terms of the contract, and when, as a consequence, the
organization deserts them, the psychological costs can be very high:
a breakdown can occur when the organization stops sending them
narcissistically gratifying signs and if they have mistaken their real
selves for their ideal ones. This breakdown can manifest itself in
different forms: serious depression, episodes of depersonalization,
burnout, and suicide attempts. All these consequences have been
studied, described, and analyzed.[13]

Envy – a direct consequence of the system

However, envy has not been described as a symptom likely to occur in
organizations that exploit the narcissistic aspects of their employees in
the "managinary" systems described above. Yet it seems to be a direct
consequence of these systems. Indeed, these organizations set their
employees into action by reawakening the infantile roots of human
behavior: the core purpose of the mechanism is to mobilize the
employees' Imaginary Register, particularly by keeping them under the

illusion of possible completeness and omnipotence. Some employees are regularly put on a pedestal and are rewarded for their efforts in trying to achieve the exceptional, the extraordinary, excellence, etc.

For example, the evaluation scale used in one big American company ranges from A to E.[14] Grade A corresponds to results that are clearly out of the ordinary, and is only exceptionally awarded "to those who have executed their responsibilities exceptionally well, who have been able to overcome the most difficult challenges, and who have displayed a level of competence and motivation that far exceeds the requirements of their positions". Generally 1 percent of the employees are awarded this grade. Grade B corresponds to results that "exceed expectations" and is awarded to 10 percent of employees. It is given to those who "have achieved a level of performance that is significantly higher than that of other employees in similar positions, who have constantly performed above and beyond what was expected of them, and have worked with true competence and motivation to overcome the most difficult challenges". This example is a good illustration of how excellence becomes an objective in itself (one that can be reached if employees invest the necessary energy) and that this excellence always implies a double referential: in relation to the others, reflected in the mirror; and in relation to the "expectations" placed on individuals.

Caught in the triangle of envy

Thus, individuals are placed in an imaginary triangle that comprises themselves, the other (the "little other" described above) – that is the one they see in the mirror, the model, the example, which is fantasmatically perceived as complete – and the Other (the "big Other") whose desires the subjects feel they must satisfy and who is embodied in the organization. The organization itself is a relatively abstract entity but one whose "demands" are real and which tends to judge, evaluate, and permanently reminds the individuals where they are supposed to "be" on the ladder, which position they should be in relation to the others, particularly those who are almost identical to themselves, and with whom they are constantly compared.

This process, as I have emphasized, helps to set individuals into action. Individuals spend their energy trying to be like this imaginary other who is constantly displayed before their eyes. But this process merely exploits envy. It is impossible for the subjects to follow their desires, as this would require that they distance themselves from the other. Here, subjects are set into action through their never-ending endeavor to be like this other, but the goalpost keeps moving and they have start over and over again.

Organizations that exploit the Imaginary Register, and trap individuals in their narcissism so that they invest their energy in the system, promote the development of envy. Or rather, *they function only because envy is at the heart of the process that sets individuals into "action"*. Desire, as an unconscious force that drives individuals, cannot be manipulated, but envy can. As mentioned earlier, certain mechanisms help to awaken and exploit it in order to push employees into action and to condition their behavior.

The damage caused by narcissism

Most of the time, envy remains concealed. Although it is the driving force behind the system, its existence is never envisaged, because mentioning it would shatter the illusion that human beings are autonomous in their actions, and that they are purely driven by a real interest in the work they perform. Yet, by exploiting envy and placing it at the heart of their management processes, organizations play a dangerous game. By reactivating the feeling of lack in the employees and by constantly exploiting their narcissistic dimension, organizations unknowingly initiate a process whose violence they often cannot control.

Killing the other

Envy has its origins in the fact that all human relations are relations between peers. By fostering envy in a social context, one also promotes the development of a bond. Indeed, envy always involves at least two people, it excludes indifference, and it acts as a kind of social "cement". However, as we explained in Chapter 2, envy creates a bond but can also destroy it; indeed envy can lead individuals to destroy and annihilate the other – the one they envy – and it can also lead them to destroy themselves. Using envy as a means of building organizations is dangerous because relations then develop on a very unhealthy basis: envy involves an envious subject and an envied *other* who is almost identical to the former. In organizations that exploit envy, the *others* are not considered in their difference and subjectivity, but in their similarity to the envious, because they can be given the role of the other in the mirror.

The Punchy example is a good illustration of this aspect. In the Punchy store we studied, it is impossible to ignore the presence of the others; the employees are reminded daily of the presence of their co-workers, and monthly of that of employees working in other Punchy stores. There is no place for indifference, and individuals cannot but be aware that they are working within a human group. In this respect, each employee is bonded to an other, but to an other that he or she wants to outmatch, crush, and even destroy. This becomes clear with the arrival of the "killer". This name was not chosen at random: the goal here is indeed to "kill" the other, first by identifying the latter and then by destroying him/her. Before her arrival in this particular store, this employee was already related to the group: people talked about her and about her results. When she arrived, the other employees positioned themselves in relation to her. The bond thus created is one that can potentially cause destruction.

Overwhelmed by one's limitations

Another problem inherent to the "managinary" system is that what drives individuals might also "crush" them. By placing models in front of their eyes, exploiting the narcissistic illusion of possible completeness is equivalent to constantly reminding the subjects of their own limitations and deficiencies. Individuals, in their attempt to fill this lack, feel caught in a stranglehold between the other as a model, and the Other's expectations, which by nature are impossible to meet. They are then in danger of being overwhelmed by their own sense of impotence and might be incapable of recovery. These are the symptoms of isolation, of feelings of worthlessness and of narcissistic suffering that we described, in Chapters 1 and 2, as being closely associated with envy.

Richard Durn or the "failed self"

Though the events in the case described below did not take place in an enterprise, they show the relation between narcissism and envy in social relations and its potentially very violent consequences. My discussion of this extreme case is based, for the most part, on the analysis proposed by clinical sociologist Vincent de Gaulejac.[15]

Case 17: **Bloodbath in Nanterre**

On the night of March 26th 2002, Richard Durn burst into the council chamber of the Paris suburb of Nanterre, shot 8 municipal councilors to death and injured 10 others. On March 28th, while in police custody, he leapt to his death from a window.

Vincent de Gaulejac's main thesis is that this tragedy is closely related to the characteristics of our "hypermodern" society, in which the ideology of self-fulfillment contains a major risk for those who cannot fulfill themselves and, as a result, have difficulty fitting into this society.

A loser of hypermodernity

Hypermodern individuals are constantly forced to acquire the qualities that are necessary to survive in today's world. Thus, they have to be mobile, reactive, efficient, responsible, autonomous, adaptable, free, capable of fulfilling their desires, etc. These requirements, communicated through schooling or education, work, or by institutions or politicians, foster an ideal of perfection and excellence that develops around a desire for omnipotence. Richard Durn is the "anti-model by excellence", the "loser of hypermodernity":[16] he is not autonomous, and neither is he flexible, responsible, or dynamic.

Although, according to his mother, he did very well at school, he failed university: it took him several years to obtain his Master's degree and he failed his exams three years in a row. Because of his lack of financial independence, he lived with his mother, he could not provide for himself, had no girlfriend, and felt incapable of projecting himself into the future. He felt trapped in an impasse. Thus, in his diaries – extracts of which were published by the French newspaper *Le Monde* – he wrote: "I am tired of finding that time passes and that I have nothing [. . .]. I can no longer stand being at the bottom of the ladder and seeing that all the people I used to know have progressed in life." Because of his complete failure to be autonomous and to fit into society (no life partner, no financial independence, no job, etc.) he found it difficult to feel alive and expressed this clearly: "I have not lived; at thirty years of age I have had no life."[17] He called himself "a coward and a moron", "a slave and weakling", considered himself "immature", and thought he had "a screw loose". He suffered from a deep feeling of inferiority and felt he lived in an existential void.

The components necessary for the development of envy can be observed here: the subject makes constant reference to the others, a reference that reminds him of his failure and which causes increasingly intolerable narcissistic suffering. His frustration keeps growing until it becomes utterly unbearable.

"Because I turned myself into a living-dead, I decided to put an end to this by killing the members of a small elite who were the symbol of and the decision makers in a city I have always loathed", he explained during his interrogation by the police,[18] soon before committing suicide. What he wrote in his diary a few weeks before he acted out his plan[19] says it all:

> The conformist I am needs to destroy lives, to do harm, so that for once in my life, I can feel alive. The taste for destruction I have developed because I have always seen and experienced myself as a good for nothing, must this time be turned against others, because I have nothing and I am nothing. [. . .] I do not deserve to live. I must die, but I want to die feeling free and having a great time. That is why I have to kill people. For once in my life I will have an orgasm. I will feel powerful, I will be somebody.

From impotence to omnipotence

Both in his diaries and during his questioning by the police, he recurrently refers to power or lack thereof. He describes himself as a complete loser, whereas what he wanted was to be above the average others, to have power and notoriety and be recognized. The illusion of an autonomous, free, powerful self – the necessary condition to "feel truly alive" – has a strong influence on him but does nothing but remind him of his own insignificance. He thinks of himself as being on a "less to more" scale, a scale supposed to represent the whole "being". Self-quantification (he describes himself as a "good for nothing"), his confusion between "having" (a status, a family, money) and "being" (in order to "be", one has to "have"), and the fact that he permanently compares what he "has" with what others have infects him with the poison of envy. The feeling of impotence and his self-disgust fosters rage; the latter grows and grows until eventually he turns it against what he considers lies at its origin. In his diaries, the themes of failure and shame are combined with that of increasing resentment for those who represent power.

"Blowing up" the triangle of envy

What he failed to achieve in life, he achieves in death: only death brings him power and notoriety; death forces "society" to recognize him, to associate his name with an image, that of a murderer. The target he selects and the time he chooses to take action are of great significance in this case. He chooses to kill city councilors at the end of a council meeting. These councilors play a double role:[20]

- That of the other, a reflection of himself, but the "positive" rather than "negative" reflection: they represent power, a power they are exercising at that precise moment in time since they are having an official meeting; this "staged" power must be destroyed;
- That of the Other (the big Other): they represent the city he loathes because he feels it has not recognized him, has not given him a place. The city represents the Other; the Other he needed recognition from.

He could have chosen to kill other representatives of power: wealthy people, entrepreneurs, etc. He chose those who, for him, represented both the other and the Other. As underlined earlier, the envious is trapped in an imaginary triangle comprising him/herself, the other (fantasmatically perceived as complete), and the Other (the mother initially, and then everything which, through a transference process, takes her place) whose desires the subject feels he/she must satisfy. But the envious subject feels incapable of satisfying the Other's needs because the other possesses what he/she needs to fill the lack in the Other. By killing the members of the city council while they were gathered at an official meeting to exercise their power, Richard Durn sought to blow up the triangle he had locked himself into.

Richard Durn was undoubtedly a psychotic and his attack was an act of folly, but this psychopathological explanation, though necessary, cannot alone account for the genesis of his action:

It allows us to find a culprit, by unloading the blame on to him. This explanation is all the more acceptable as his life was filled with serious disorders – instability, depression, suicide attempts, marginality – which were all symptoms of his difficulties of existence. But these symptoms also reveal the contradictions of our world. Richard Durn experienced himself as a complete failure, as the typical example of self-unfulfillment, the reversed reflection of which reveals a social demand: each subject is confronted with the necessity of fulfilling him/herself, and this self-fulfillment depends on recognition by others.[21]

This extreme example helps highlight the role of the social system in the development of this pathology. When the system is governed by the ideology of self-fulfillment, with the demand for excellence, power, and autonomy it implies, it runs the risk of being *overcome by an uncontrollable wave of envy, particularly among those for whom the psychological cost of the gap between themselves and the ideal or model is too high.*

Noemie, or the narcissistic collapse

The story of Richard Durn, though it helps us understand the links between systems that are based essentially on the mobilization of the subjects' Imaginary Register and the development of envy, is an extreme example and takes place within a social context but outside the workplace. I shall now present a case that takes place in a hypermodern enterprise.

Case 18: From passionate investment to collapse[22]
Noemie, after completing her tertiary education, is hired by the French subsidiary of a multinational company which operates according to the modern organization principles described above, principles through which the company gains a psychological hold over its employees via the mobilization of their Imaginary Register. For nine years, Noemie fully complies with the system for which she works relentlessly, sometimes seven days a week. Her commitment to her job is intense and rests on an implicit narcissistic contract between her company and herself: in return for a behavior oriented towards progress and success, as defined by the organization through certain criteria, the latter offers Noemie recognition, a sense of belonging and appreciation. Noemie finds herself captured in the Imaginary dimension. There no longer is any intermediary between herself and the almighty organization (the Other in the sense meant by Lacan), an organization that

presents her with a highly positive image of herself with which she fully identifies.

"When you start working there, you have to give yourself entirely to the system, to the organization. In any case, as a manager, you have no choice, you have to operate this way; those who don't are very quickly set aside," Noemie later said when she described her experience. *"This organization really grinds you, eats you . . . it does this through some kind of corporate ethic or culture that tells us that we're the best, with the slogan: "you're the most beautiful, the greatest, the strongest". You must excel in everything, it's in your contract . . . it's excellence through excellence . . . Every two months they immerse you again in the theme of excellence; there's a whole series of training programs, seminars . . . They send you to a beautiful place and for a week they remind you of the objectives, of why you are there, of what you must do and that every little thing you do is important for the organization."*[23]

"You have to be the best, the most perfect; every note, every document talks about perfection; the top management team and the human resources directors regularly – every two days on average – send notes about the notion of perfection, about the demands we must make of ourselves and of clients."[24]

After a few years, the company undergoes major organizational changes that have important consequences for Noemie: it expands from 400 to 2000 employees, is reorganized, and Noemie loses a good deal of the autonomy she once enjoyed. But it is a conflict that arises between one of her colleagues and herself that upsets Noemie more than anything else. As a result of the company's reorganization, her colleague, who used to work at the same level as hers in the hierarchy, becomes her direct superior. *"We had different ways of seeing things . . . but as long as we were equals, it worked pretty well. After he was promoted though, he wanted to make me fold and I really struggled with it . . . But what hurt me the most was the fact that they chose this guy who had never done anything remarkable. In times of need and when there were problems, he wasn't there. When we needed to solve potentially disastrous crises, he wasn't there. He only emerged when everything was OK . . . So when an organization like this one selects a guy like him . . . well I guess I felt really confused . . . Through him I had a passionate relationship with the organization, and in fact by blaming him, I was blaming this organization, which promises you things . . . and then you never get them . . ."*[25]

It then became more and more difficult for Noemie to go to work. She started crying often, felt demotivated, until one day she broke down entirely: *"The day when everything flipped . . . it was quite dramatic because people had always seen me as a lively, strong, dignified person, and that day I completely collapsed. I remember very well . . . I was in my office, I walked in, dropped my bag and then I broke into uncontrollable tears. I felt . . . it was worse than if I had been standing in front of a dead person . . . worse than if a very dear friend or relative had been lying dead before me. I couldn't stop. And then my whole self-image broke . . . it was as if I had grabbed someone standing there and broken him or her."*[26]

One could not express more clearly on what the exchange between the company and Noemie was based. The latter is kept under the illusion of an ideal, omnipotent ego she mistakes for her real self, which results in her complete alienation from the company, a company from which she expects to receive love and recognition. In more Lacanian terms, the company plays the role of the Other, also perceived as complete and omnipotent and whom the subject must satisfy entirely.

The company's reorganization, an event Noemie identifies as the beginning of her breakdown, triggers a process of de-idealization that leads to a serious depression. As a result, Noemie spends four months in a psychiatric hospital and then resigns from the company, feeling this is the only way to "survive".

Nicole Aubert and Vincent de Gaulejac's analysis of this case is based mostly on concepts borrowed from the psychoanalytical theory of the *Ideal Ego,* and shows how this type of organization provides the subjects with a personality support, with the reassurance that they exist, that they are worth something. It is then the "anxiety to lose the object" that threatens the person, because "without the object", the person might fall into depression. This is exactly what happens in Noemie's case when she loses the support of the organization and when this loss leads to the collapse and loss of her Ideal Ego. She then sinks into acute depression, a process during which she is forced to face this loss, without, initially, being able to overcome it."[27]

When the organization turns its gaze away

What is particularly interesting in this case is what Noemie describes as the turning point, the moment when an other, with whom, up till then, she had been an equal, suddenly becomes her direct superior. What deeply hurts her, and above all triggers the breakdown process, is the fact that "an organization like this one selects a guy like him". Here, we have a situation where the other (the colleague, who until now was the subject's equal), presented in the mirror, is fantasmatically perceived as suddenly stealing the Other's (i.e. the organization's) gaze. The subject (Noemie) then loses the support upon which she entirely depends to exist, one which she cannot let go of: the Other's gaze, support, and desire which gave her the illusion that she was complete and omnipotent. Without the Other's gaze, the subject is at risk of finding herself in the pre-mirror stage, a stage during which she felt like a body in pieces. This is what Noemie expresses when she says: "[. . .] my whole self-image broke . . . it was as if I had grabbed someone standing there and broken him or her." Not only does the organization take its gaze away from Noemie, but it also turns it onto an other. We are here at the heart of the process of envy, a triangular process involving Noemie, the Other (the organization), and the other (the colleague), who by stealing the Other's gaze, love, and attention deprives the subject of the ideal self-image with which the Other had initially presented her. It is at that precise moment that Noemie is confronted with an inner void and by the feeling of no longer existing.

Noemie's comments provide a good illustration of the mechanisms involved in envy. On the one hand, Noemie tries to deny the worth of her colleague (he is not good, the organization is making a mistake, etc.) by belittling him. She clashes with him. Yet, according to her, when they were "equals" everything went well. Examined from the perspective of envy, Noemie's comments are logical: she expresses the hostility and hatred triggered in her by the sight of this rival whom she feels is depriving her of the organization's gaze and therefore love. She symbolically attempts to make him disappear by belittling him. On the other hand, she cannot help feeling that she has failed and makes her own (what she interprets as the organization's) verdict about herself: she is not promoted because she is not good enough, she is not worthy enough. Two symptoms associated with envy can be observed here:

- Aggressiveness towards the other, the double in the mirror, the sight of whom she cannot bear because it reminds her of her own incompleteness;
- Isolation and depression when the subject is "crushed" by the feeling of being worthless, of no longer existing, of being transparent to the Other's gaze, a gaze that is now turned onto an other.

As Lacan suggested, a subject suffering from envy is a person on the brink of collapse, of disappearance.

Detaching oneself from the other

To better understand what happens in Noemie's case, let us take the example of the professor who learns that his friend and colleague has been offered a post in a better university. In this case also there is a triangle of envy: the subject, the other (the colleague who plays the role of the double in the mirror), and the Other (the university system with its own appreciation rules). When he hears the news, the professor initially feels envious, but he progressively detaches himself from the other (his colleague) and from the Other (the university system), thus freeing himself from the triangle that had allowed envy to take hold of him. Realizing and acknowledging that he is feeling envious, he enters into a process of self-reflection, the objective of which is to understand the gap that has suddenly appeared between himself and the other, an other he thought was alike to him. Rather than holding on to the idea that the other is his double – but one who, unlike him, possesses that "little something" which he needs to take his place – he tries to interpret this gap. One possible interpretation is that other, the one who was supposed to be "almost similar" to the subject, is actually not all that similar to the latter. The subject must then try to understand what the differences are; this can lead the person to realize what is really important to him/her: "Yes, I would also like to have this post, but on the other hand, the reason why I gave up the idea a few years ago was because I knew what the costs would be: much more pressure, less time for myself and with my family."

Feeling envious and acknowledging it can help envious individuals to take stock of themselves and recognize the ambivalence they feel about their professional projects: all choices come with a price and all changes imply gains and losses. By being able to identify what they gave up when they made those choices, and understand why they gave up what they did, they can form a more accurate perception of themselves. They can then better understand what they have gained by distancing themselves from a system that encourages certain types of behavior. Renouncing certain things can be interpreted as self-assertion, in so far as it implies that the person depart from the criteria the system uses to determine the value of individuals, that he or she detach him/herself from the "other in the mirror", who is successful in the system, and that he/she develops a professional project founded on more self-respect. This self-reflection process enables individuals to progressively erase and eliminate envy, by untying the binds that would otherwise have kept them captive in the triangle of envy formed by themselves, the other, and the Other.

Noemie, on the contrary, cannot escape from this triangle. She cannot even start to look at things from a different perspective in that she is probably incapable of recognizing the seeds of envy that have sprouted within her – for good reasons since the system has occulted this dimension, even though (or because) it is based on this triangle. Noemie's case is, in my opinion, emblematic of the effects of the type of relationships that form between individuals and management systems of organizations that exploit their employees' Imaginary Register.

Narcissism and envy in traditional organizations

Certain organizations, which existed long before the hypermodern ones we have discussed in this chapter, knew how to exploit the narcissistic side that potentially existed in all individuals, in order to cause their members to almost entirely lose their identity to the system's cause. Already, those traditional organizations could find themselves ravaged by uncontrollable waves of envy, when the mechanism on which the organization relied to ensure that all its members invested body and soul in the system ran out of control.

Case 19: **Envy at the convent**
Studies of life in a convent have shown that envy could arise between nuns and lead to extreme violence in certain communities. Confinement, punishments, cruelty, deprivation of care, emotional

abuse, poisoning, accusations of witchcraft, etc. could in certain cases result from envy.[28] There are even examples of communities that were eventually dissolved when the outrageous violence that prevailed in them was finally exposed.

Several characteristics of convents and of how they function can help us understand how envy develops. Firstly, "it is an enclosed space, in which human relations are confined to a small circle of people, from which it is almost impossible to escape. It is also a world where every aspect of life is ruled by time, activities are strictly controlled, and where as a result the most mundane things of everyday life can be turned into events that have serious consequences".[29] In this closed universe, a level of uniformity governs life: women only live with women; mothers superior, novice mistresses, etc. are elected to their posts for a temporary period; prayer and fasting obligations and daily chores are equally distributed. In some orders, the nuns even have to exchange personal clothes and items so that they do not get too attached to them. These characteristics are common to many, religious or non-religious, communities, in which indifferentiation is at the foundation of the constitution of the group. As I explained at the beginning of Chapter 4 with the example of Kibbutzim, such organizations erase differences and promote evenness, and in doing so create the perfect breeding ground for envy.

However, another characteristic can explain the violent eruption of this emotion. Indeed, convents are enclosed places governed by very powerful emulation principles:

> In a convent, all women normally have the same goal: working on perfecting themselves in order to receive the Divine Blessing, and at the same time, others' recognition. But only a few of them achieve this goal, and in so doing generate envy in the others. The latter, to defend themselves, belittle the saint's image, deny her virtues and spiritual graces, and in fact accuse her of consorting with the devil [. . .]. The saint also conspires against the others, whom she deems insufficiently devout and obedient, claiming that she can read their mind and influence their fate through her prayers.[30]

In a convent, the narcissistic dimension is at the heart of the relation that binds the individual to her community:

> The game starts with an obstinate and egocentric quest for inner perfection that must lead to a privileged relationship with the Divine spouse. The game is all the more cruel and perverse as it is the most mortified and the most humble who receives the best place and her behavior is presented to the others as an example to follow. What's more, despite your efforts to achieve this ideal, God, for reasons you cannot grasp, might eventually grant his grace to someone else, though you do not feel that this choice is objectively justifiable.[31]

Here again we observe the triangular relationship that generates envy: the relation to the other, who is all the more comparable to the subject as she is the same sex, lives in identical conditions, has the same rights and the same duties; and the relationship to the Other, here represented by the "Divine spouse" by whom the subject seeks to be recognized so that she can then be recognized by the others. It is all the more difficult to free oneself from this triangle as a convent is a closed community that lives in quasi autarky. When envy explodes, the damage it can cause is difficult to control and can lead to the destruction of the community.

From Narcissus to Nemesis

From the perspective developed in this chapter, envy is considered as the "other side of the coin" in organizations where individuals are encouraged onto the path of narcissism. The latter manifests itself through an unending race for excellence, for more, for self-perfection, while the organization constantly reminds its members of their position in this race, in relation to the others, and of what they must aim for. The image of the other, of the model, presented to the subjects in the mirror, is essential to the process through which the individuals invest themselves entirely in the organization. This implies a form of emulation and competition, but results in an almost inevitable development of envy. There is then a shift from Narcissus to Nemesis, the Greek symbol of envy.

The existence of envy reveals the extreme fragility of these systems; systems that rest on the fragility of their members, whose sense of identity is made vulnerable by their inability to overcome narcissistic doubt. Even when they are successful, success is relative, and just as in Punchy's case, the subjects might plunge to the bottom of the performance chart even though they were in top position for a while. Their quest can never end. Success, if there is any, is only momentary. As we said earlier, envy is a poison, but it is a poison that infects a system long before its consequences can be perceived. Indeed, it is easy to spot envy when it is associated with the patent failure of individuals, with their inability to succeed according to the criteria set out by the organization or by society, and it is easy to identify once it has caused violence or a serious nervous breakdown that requires psychiatric treatment. But in most cases, envy lurks, invisible, in the heart of the system, ready to pounce on those who seem successful. The moment the quest for success is dictated by a narcissistic relation to the other, the worm is in the fruit.

In Chapter 4, I have shown how contemporary organizations, by using management tools that enable them to systematize and stage the comparison of employees with one another, were likely to be breeding grounds for envy. And because these evolutions are now common to most, small or large, private or public, organizations, envy is an emotion that is likely to emerge in most of them, as an unwanted and often concealed consequence of their management practices.

In this chapter I have placed emphasis on hypermodern organizations whose management techniques all work together to enable the organizations to gain a powerful psychological hold over their employees by trapping them in their own desires of narcissistic assertion. In a hypermodern organization, envy is used to mobilize employees and push them to engage in the internal competition. Envy then becomes more than a consequence of the management system; it is now part and parcel of the mechanism. And yet it presents the paradox of never being talked about or acknowledged, because admitting its existence would be equivalent to destroying the very mechanism on which the organization relies to ensure the involvement and commitment of its employees. It is in those cases that envy is likely to have the most devastating consequences, particularly by leading to serious attacks on the system or by contributing to the psychological breakdown of individuals.

However, we can make the hypothesis that these organizations attract a specific type of employee: those whose psychological make-up suits their management systems, and for whom narcissistic questioning is difficult to overcome. In these cases, envy is not just an episode that occurs once during their professional career, it is the driving force behind the latter. The long-term consequences of such a scenario can be disastrous when the organization on which these employees depend for narcissistic support abandons them, when the employees start showing signs of weakness, or when reorganization leads to an unfavorable redistribution of positions.

Card 4   What should I do if I am envious of someone who, I feel, has been more successful than myself?

If you are capable of asking yourself this question: WELL DONE! You have the courage to identify this emotion as envy and to express your feelings. This is essential in order to be able to move forward and to let go of the negative feelings you have towards this person (anger, silent hatred, resentment, agitation, a need to belittle the person, the inability to work with him or her, etc.) or towards yourself (sadness, discouragement, a feeling of failure, of inferiority, etc.).

Try and gain some perspective on all this, so that you can define what, in the other, triggers your envy: on what precise points is your envy focused? Is it the fact that the other person was promoted? Is it the fact that he/she successfully completed a project? Is it his/her education level? And so on.

Now, take another close look at yourself: what do these precise points reveal about your own experience? What does this echo? They reveal certain aspects of your experience that remain painful: a particular failure, an ideal you used to have and that you have not been able to achieve, a more general feeling that you're not up to the job, etc. It is these points that you must work on: why has it been so difficult for you to accept this particular failure? Or failure in general? Where did this demanding ideal come from? Why do you hold on to it if it prevents you from enjoying the positive aspects of your career?

Take this opportunity to think about your history. Think again about the reasons why you made certain choices rather than others. Think also of the more general context in which you have evolved: what are your life choices? What has helped/hindered you in your career? What are you proud of? Have you ever been surprised to discover new resources in yourself? When?

You are progressively going to take possession of your own history: it is yours and it cannot be compared to anybody else's; it has brought you satisfactions but also difficulties, joys but also failures; it is rich and complex. It only belongs to you.

You might still feel a little envy, but it will be appeased and you will be more detached from it. If it re-emerges, start the exercise again and take the opportunity to explore new aspects.

Identifying envy within oneself gives you the opportunity to know yourself better. Make the most of it!

6

Situations that can Trigger Envy

In the previous chapters, I have shown how organizational systems and management methods could contribute to a more or less damaging development of envy. The problem we drew attention to was the fact that when envy becomes a central component of the way an organization functions, its effects can be destructive. However, organizations do not all function like those described in Chapters 4 and 5. Envy is not always as systematic and deep-seated as it is in the examples I gave earlier. It can occur, but must then be seen as a production of the system at a given time, rather than as a permanent dimension of the latter. The challenge is then to be able to identify the events or moments, during organizational life, which are likely to trigger envy.

Emotions are inevitable in the workplace

Life at work is impregnated with emotions.[1] They can be discrete or violent, negative or positive, they can be experienced by an entire team or by one person, and they can be felt repeatedly or very occasionally. However they manifest themselves, emotions are omnipresent in organizations and impact on many decision-making processes and actions.[2] Indeed, it would be quite surprising if people could set aside their emotions eight hours a day and five days a week! What is more, many people develop their identity as individuals in the workplace and therefore invest themselves emotionally in their work. Generally speaking, work implies close and frequent interactions between people and high levels of interdependence that are likely to generate various types of emotions.

Some of these emotions are light and positive and make work more pleasant. Thus, when there is a nice atmosphere between team workers and when humor is used appropriately,[3] or when employees feel appreciated as individuals by an understanding manager, the work experience is more likely to be satisfactory. But work can also be associated with painful and negative emotions. Individuals can, for example, feel anger, frustration, bitterness, disgust, sadness, stress, or envy.[4]

In some cases, these emotions have their origins outside the workplace: an employee might have been told that he/she is suffering from a serious illness, or he/she might have to take some leave in order to take care of a sick child or parent; another employee might be having relational difficulties with a member of his/her family, or the roof of his/her house might be leaking; and transport issues can also make access to work difficult. In all cases, even though these events take place outside work, the resulting emotions have consequences at work: employees cannot switch off their emotions and leave them outside the office door. Their emotions affect their colleagues, either indirectly through empathy or by an effect of contagion, or directly because of a change in their behavior.

But work can also, and frequently, be the direct cause of unpleasant or painful emotions. A member of a team or a manager might find that their behavior is misunderstood by the people who work with them. The reorganization of a company has consequences for the number of posts and on the distribution of work. A client cancels an important meeting at the last minute. The absence of an employee impacts on a whole department. An employee is injured at work. The results of the company are not as good as expected. Many more examples could be given. All organizations and all types of work environments are places where unpleasant events, to a greater or lesser degree, occur daily and are likely to generate negative emotions. What is surprising is that in most cases these emotions are dealt with by the system as they arise and are not allowed to "fester".

Toxic emotions in organizations

But there are also cases when the organization is, or becomes, unable to manage and eliminate these emotions. This is when the latter can turn toxic:[5] the body produces toxins, which, most of the time it is capable of eliminating naturally, but which can make it sick if it no longer manages to evacuate them. In the same way, an organization produces emotions, which, if not dealt with, can truly affect its functioning. The emotions then become toxic, they absorb people's energy, and sometimes that of the whole system. Instead of concentrating their efforts on productive actions, individuals spend their time fighting against the noxious effects of these emotions, or worse, end up amplifying them. They become incapable of dealing effectively with the problems they are facing. Allowing emotions to fester can impact negatively on the turnover, the rate of absenteeism, the health of employees, and the creativity and performance of work teams.

Envy is a good candidate for toxicity. It is no coincidence that it is often described as a "poison" or "venom" that gradually and ineluctably penetrates the system, sometimes with disastrous consequences. And it is because envy is often concealed that it can become toxic. Most emotions, such as anger or sadness, are visible and can be expressed by people. They are therefore easier to identify; and it is because they are identifiable that they can be taken into account and dealt with. Envy, on the contrary, and as mentioned earlier, is a shameful, taboo, hidden, and often unconscious emotion, and it is expressed in a disguised way. For example, it can manifest itself in the form of aggressiveness towards a person, and yet it might be impossible to know with certainty that this aggressiveness is caused by envy. What makes it so toxic is the fact that its presence is concealed and disguised: it is difficult to spot at first and, just like a mushroom that grows slowly but surely in the shadow of a tree, it can develop all the more freely as it is not identified.

Typology of situations that may give rise to envy

It is important to be aware of moments or events in organizational life during which envy might arise, although the organization and its management methods might not, in themselves, be pathological in nature. Certain circumstances can trigger envy; being able to recognize them and knowing that they can generate envy helps in managing them in appropriate ways. The challenge is not to eradicate envy – indeed envy is an emotion that is almost inevitable in society and particularly at work – but rather to manage the circumstances or events that are likely to generate envy in such a way that it is not allowed to grow out of proportion, which would make it truly toxic and dangerous for the entire system or part of it.

In most organizations, there are "toxin handlers",[6] who serve as therapists, often without being aware of it, and help to eliminate the toxins. They identify, deal with, and neutralize potentially toxic situations so that their colleagues can refocus their attention on constructive action. Managers play an essential role in this process: the onus is on them to ensure that their decisions and actions do not generate long-lasting toxic emotions that might become too deepseated for the system to eliminate and that might end up poisoning it. With regard to envy, it is essential that managers be aware of the situations, circumstances, or management decisions that can potentially stimulate this emotion.

The cases of envy described by a number of authors, and the studies I have conducted in different types of organizations (a university, a retail group, interim and consultancy agencies, a regional agency of a paragovernmental organization, a hospital, etc.) lead me to group these situations into two categories:

1 When the places of individuals within the organization are changed or interchanged: as a result of reorganizations, for example, or of more common human resources management decisions related to recruitment or to career management;
2 When the members of a team, a service, or an organization become overly interdependent: when budget allocation decisions are being made or when the skills of one employee become essential to another and as a result brings out a weakness.

I shall discuss these two categories of situations in the two following sections.

When the places of individuals change

As underlined in Chapter 4, the question of individuals' places is fundamental in the problematic of envy. An envious individual is fascinated by the other, by the place the latter occupies, and which the envious perceives as enviable, or at least more enviable than his own. Envy emerges in subjects who are caused to imagine that they can or should be in someone else's place, but are not. The other's place is enviable, because it gives the latter access to something that the envious individual does not possess: in an organization, this "something" might be power, a better salary (or rewards), or status. It is enviable also because it is the concrete manifestation of the fact that the other has distinguished him/herself to the system: at a given time he/she was chosen for this place. He/she has drawn and continues to draw the attention of the system, whereas the envious subject might feel dispossessed and unappreciated by the system.

As explained in Chapter 5, the issue of individuals' places is rooted in archaic processes that took place in the earliest phase of their development: the mirror phase, a process during which a child finally identifies to the "other in the mirror", providing the "Other" (often the mother) recognizes him/her and confirms that it is indeed him/herself that he/she sees in this image. In envy, envious subjects are once again trapped in this triangular configuration that comprises the one they see in the mirror, the model, the example which they fantasmatically perceive as complete, and the Other whose gaze they need to capture. In the context of work, the Other can be embodied in the organization or a manager: the Other has "expectations", tends to judge, evaluate, and constantly reminds the individual of his/her position in relation to others. In this configuration, the place of each individual and the imaginary relations that link these places are clearly defined.

In Chapters 4 and 5, I showed how some systems promote triangular relationships of this type and in doing so contribute to develop envy as an integral part of how they function.

In the case of Punchy, for example, the hierarchical structure of the store is very simple: there is a management team that consists of only two people and a team of salespeople in which the places of individuals are interchangeable. The boundaries separating the different departments no longer exist and the performance evaluations conducted and displayed daily by the director show that the employees' positions are short-lived. This permanent instability reinforces in the employees the idea that they can take each other's place. Each individual is a potential mirror reflection of an other; as for the director, he plays the role of the "Other", whose attention and gaze the subjects need to capture. There is, in this case, a wide array of triangular relationships: between each salesperson, each of his/her "quasi doubles", and the director.

In the case of the business school, the reorganization results in the "new recruits" taking the place of the "seniors", when the former are given not only the roles but also the offices that used to belong to the "seniors". Here again the individuals are caught in a triangular relationship between the director, the "new recruits", and the "seniors".

In both these cases, the system explicitly and permanently plays with the issue of places, which contributes to the development of envy. What we need to do now is to identify the situations, at work, in which individuals' places within their organization change and are defined through a triangular relationship, *without the management system necessarily being unhealthy.*

Organizational change and redistribution of roles

Most organizations undergo regular changes, during which their structure, processes, and modes of functioning are more or less radically modified. Such changes are often inevitable and necessary. However, in many cases, changes fail to achieve the desired improvement and more often than not lead to fiascos. Very often, the cause of the failure is not so much what the change was supposed to accomplish, but rather how the process of change was conducted.

Change and emotions

It has now been recognized that change[7] could generate strong and often negative emotions,[8] which, if not acknowledged and dealt with, can become a real obstacle to change. Organizational transformation cannot be considered a purely rational and logical process: many people are involved in this process and they react to it emotionally and psychologically.

At first, the announcement of change causes individuals to feel uncertain and insecure about their jobs and professional future. What will their future work conditions be? Will they be treated fairly by the organization? Will their past investments be taken into account? Furthermore, any change, even when it is "positive" or "logical", implies a loss. Individuals must give up the way things were done in the "old organization", the position they previously occupied, their old habits, and often colleagues with whom they had developed good relationships. The past must always be left behind and buried. More generally, many individuals experience change as a profound modification of the contract that bonds them, often implicitly and psychologically, to their organization. It therefore seems obvious that resistance to change can only be overcome if the emotions and feelings experienced by the individuals concerned are acknowledged and taken into account.

Among all these emotions, one is particularly likely to emerge during organizational change: yes, you guessed right – envy.

Will there be a place for me?

Out of all the questions employees ask themselves, those related to their own place are the most important: will there be a place for me in the future organization? If yes, where? Where will the others be? Organizational change brings out the components of the triangular relation discussed earlier.

Employees who know they are going to be moved to new positions are placed in a situation of high dependence upon the "big Other" (the organization, its leaders, or those who make decisions and manage change), from whom the verdict must come. In most cases, employees do not have the power to decide where they will go and what they will do in the transformed organization. They feel that they depend on the goodwill of the decision-makers, who are sometimes perceived as omnipotent. This places them in a position of rather infantile dependence and jeopardizes their sense of autonomy.

As for the image of the "other", the one reflected in the mirror, it is reactivated: individuals cannot but be aware that their own places are not guaranteed and that they might be compared to other people whose profiles are comparable to theirs. They might be selected or discarded. They might perceive their new position as a failure if compared to the one they previously occupied, and to the one the other has acquired. This reactivation of a triangular relation (the subject, the other, and the Other) is more than likely to promote envy.

Fear of not being up to the job

The feeling of vulnerability an employee can experience during a reorganization process increases the risks of envy. Indeed, any change requires new competencies, which causes much anxiety: will I be able to change? Will I be able to cope with the new situation? Will I be able to adapt? Such questions lead to self-doubt and reveal one's own limitations. The subjects might feel inferior to other people with whom they are compared. And as it happens, envy is closely associated with feelings of inferiority, with a difficulty to accept one's own limitations, and with a lack of self-esteem. The prospect of change at work is therefore all the more likely to generate emotions like envy in such individuals.

Incidentally, it was while I was providing consultancy services to firms undergoing organizational change that I realized that the reactions I observed in people could only be explained by one thing: the existence of envy. When the announcement of change is made, some of the most asked questions are: "What will become of me?" "Where will such or such a colleague go?" "On what basis are employees selected?" "Why has X been appointed to position Y?" Most people spontaneously assume that they are going to lose something in this change, and when we take a closer look at this aspect, it becomes clear that they do feel that they will lose something, and that others ("shareholders", "directors", "X") will gain. The anxiety among individuals is first of all related to the fear of losing their place in the system, which always means, more or less implicitly, that other people will take their place. This anxiety is the residue of an archaic fear (archaic in that it takes roots in a very infantile part of our psyche): the subjects have a fantasmatic fear of no longer existing in the eyes of their mother, whose gaze might turn onto an other, who will then be envied by the subjects. This is why, during organizational change, the issue of the employees' places, and of the loss associated with the change, is likely to cause strong, but repressed, feelings of envy in people. When people are reassured about their future place, they are more willing and able to cooperate in the change or to accept it with serenity.

***Case 20:* The TotalFina–Elf merger and the rule of parity**
In the year 2000, when the French oil company TotalFina took over its competitor Elf,[9] the top management decided to merge the two organizations. The creation of the new organization was based, explicitly, on the so-called "principle of parity": all new teams had to comprise an equal number of ex-TotalFina employees and ex-Elf employees. Responsibilities were also distributed equally between the two groups of employees and members of both companies were appointed in equal numbers to management positions.

The top management justified the use of this rule considering that it would allow for a "fair" distribution of jobs and responsibilities, which would alleviate fears – particularly among Elf employees – that they would lose a lot as a result of this reorganization.

The fact that the rule of parity was used implicitly indicates that the management recognized that envy could be at the origin of resistance to change. The aim was therefore to avoid triggering off envy by setting up conditions that would help keep it in check.

Too often, resistance to change is interpreted as being related to the fear of losing power. This hypothesis underestimates the psychological implications of organizational change for individuals affected by this change. Indeed, the hypothesis of the loss of power supposes that the only thing individuals can think of is to extend their influence. The hypothesis of envy, on the other hand, introduces a degree of relativity and the question of the other: the comparison with others, rather than self-comparison, takes over. It is no so much the loss of power in itself that individuals fear, but rather the idea that they might lose something and that an other will gain, an other whom the subjects fantasmatically perceive as "complete", and unaffected by loss.

The place of the other in recruitment

Recruitment is never innocuous: introducing a new person into a team always presents the risk of disrupting the balance established in the relations between the members of the group. The phase following the recruitment of one or several people is often tricky because it corresponds to a time when envy might emerge or grow among individuals.

Recruiting two people who are too alike

In the case of Fanny and Cecilia (Case 5), both performing their on-the-job training at the purchase center of a large retail group, Fanny had already started her training course when Cecilia was recruited. The latter's arrival triggered strong feelings of envy in Fanny, feelings that were at the roots of her hostility toward Cecilia, but also of her self-isolation and her paralyzing fear of failing. Fanny's psychological characteristics are partly the cause of her envy.

However, the circumstances also contributed to its development, and this is what we shall discuss now. Fanny started feeling envious as soon as Cecilia was recruited. The latter, because of her characteristics and the place she was attributed, suddenly appeared in Fanny's mirror. Indeed, Cecilia was very similar to Fanny: they had the same gender, same qualifications, and were the same age. They were given similar training posts, in the same section of the store (but in different departments). The two trainees were expected to work together, and their missions were identical. The organizational context therefore played a significant role in triggering envy in Fanny: when two almost similar people are recruited and expected to work side by side, comparison between the two is inevitable. Cecilia's recruitment came as a surprise for Fanny, whereas Cecilia applied for the post knowing that her friend already had a job in the organization. Cecilia did not feel envious of Fanny, which shows that the context alone cannot explain the existence of envy. But it does play a part in triggering it when the subject, because of his/her psychological make-up, is prone to envy.

Fanny's envy decreased significantly when the two students were separated as a result of a reorganization of the store. Here is what she wrote about her evolution:

> Thanks to the move, I found myself at the heart of the gardening department, besides assistants and buyers. [. . .] It was then that I really started integrating myself in the team and asserting myself. This move enabled me to "rebuild myself" so to speak. This period coincided with an improvement in my relationship with Cecilia. The geographical distance the move created between her and myself enabled me to look at things from a different perspective and reinforced my desire to assert myself.

The context now had the inverse effect: it placed the two students at enough distance from each other, and reduced the mirror effect that affected Fanny when she was working with Cecilia. From then on Fanny stops feeling envious.

Who will take the boss's place?

The following case takes place in the human resources management department of a company employing one hundred and fifty people.

Case 21: A face to face that turns sour[10]

This department comprises eight employees supervised by one manager. Out of these eight employees, seven are "seniors": they are women in their forties with low levels of qualifications and who have been working in the department for at least 10 years. The eighth employee, Frederic, is a man whose profile is very different to that of his colleagues: he is 26 and has a Masters Degree in management. He has been in this department for two years and worked as a recruiter for a consultancy firm before joining this company. He was recruited as an administrative employee. The department's manager, Caroline, is also an administrative employee and is aged 37.

Relations between the members of the department are reasonably good, until Caroline goes on parental leave. A person is recruited to help the team, but not to replace Caroline. Caroline's direct superior, the administrative and financial director of the company, whose office is located on a different storey of the building, is temporarily put in charge of the department; but he does not manage the team, and in effect his role is to sign documents.

The new recruit, Isabelle, is 24 and is a business school graduate with a specialization in human resources management. She previously worked for one year in another firm. She is recruited by this firm as an administrative employee. A few weeks after her arrival, the relations between Isabelle and Frederic become strained, which causes efficiency to drop in the department: the decisions he makes contradict hers and vice versa, they are incapable of collaborating, and they each try to rally the rest of the team against the other.

After a few months, the relations between the employees and the work atmosphere deteriorate to such a degree that several employees ask to be transferred to other departments. Alarmed, the administrative and financial director decides to use the services of a consultant to solve the conflict.

Interviews with all the members of the team showed that the roots of the conflict lay in the relationship between Isabelle and Frederic. Frederic struggled with the arrival of his colleague: he considered that she was very similar to him in terms of professional characteristics, and until she was recruited he was the only employee with such a profile in the department. The fact that Isabelle had a specialization in human resources management and that his own qualifications

were more "general" seemed to have induced in him a sense of inse-
curity about his own abilities. As for Isabelle, she very quickly became
aware of Frederic's hostility towards her, which spurred her to compete with him.

What's more, the sudden absence of an authority and the relative
ambiguity in the roles of both employees led them to position themselves as potential managers of the department. Because the image of
one was constantly reflected in the other's mirror, they were both
swept into what René Girard calls "the spiral of double mimesis": the
moment the possibility of taking the boss's place becomes desirable
to one, it becomes desirable to the other, which further enhances the
desirability of this position. Each subject contributes to the emergence of the other as a rival.

The solution put in place in this case, once the fundamental origins of this conflict were identified, consisted of separating the two
protagonists, by clearly defining Isabelle's responsibilities so as to
enable her to work autonomously. She was put in charge of recruitment and of recruitment only, while Frederic was placed in charge of
training and career management. As for the team manager's functions, they were performed by a person who was recruited on a temporary basis for this specific purpose. Her professional profile differed
from Isabelle's and Frederic's: she was older and had solid experience
in team management.

In this case, the context played a significant role in generating
envy and rivalry, by permanently placing in each other's mirrors two
people with very similar profiles, who had to work side by side and
who, as a result, were constantly under each other's gaze. The
absence of a manager and of external authority pushed the pair even
deeper into the spiral of envy.

In both the cases described above, the recruitment of a new
employee activates envy. Two factors contribute to this development:
on the one hand the person recruited is too similar to another member of the team, and on the other, the context is such that each pro-
tagonist is constantly aware of the other's reflection in his/her mirror.

Generational envy

Another case that frequently occurs in organizations concerns the fears
that can arise in the minds of older employees. Such individuals feel
anxious at the prospect of working with people who are younger than

they are and have higher qualifications, and who as a result might take their place or reveal their limitations. In some cases, it is envy that causes these reactions: youth, education, and talent in others can remind people of their own limitations and deficiencies. The other, because he/she is younger or more highly qualified, suddenly projects in the mirror a characteristic of the subject which the latter cannot bear, and which he/she would rather forget. People who have found satisfaction in their career, who are not plagued by unexpressed frustration, who feel they still have the potential to progress in their career, and who have accepted their own limitations will probably not feel envious of younger, gifted people. Subjects who, on the contrary, lack self-confidence get caught in the illusion that the others are complete beings who have not yet been confronted with their own limitations; in this case envy is likely to emerge. The mere presence of the others can revive the pain caused by past failures and might cause the subjects to wish pain on the others. This is what some call generational envy.[11]

Envying one's subordinates

Generational envy can take different forms. For example, when senior managers have to retire but cannot bear the idea that a younger manager is going to take their position, they might be tempted to do everything in their power to block their successor's career, instead of training the latter and transmitting their knowledge. When leaders envy their subordinates – who still have long careers ahead of them – they might disguise their envy by frequently complaining about having to do all the work and not being appropriately rewarded for their efforts, whereas their collaborators do precious little and get well paid for it. The chances of them giving encouragement to and congratulating the people they work with are also quite slim.[12]

The envious recruiter

Generational envy can also emerge during recruitment processes. An envious recruiter might take advantage of his/her position to put obstacles in the path of a candidate he/she envies, thus preventing the latter from obtaining what he/she covets. Strangely enough, this dimension of recruitment is never talked about. Recruiters are supposed to be able to maintain enough objective distance between themselves and the people they interview; they do not feel the need to compare themselves to the others, or if they do, they should be able to look at them with indulgence because they are alike. In practice, however, this is not always the case: the more "comparable" and compared the other is to the recruiter, the more the latter's regrets and limitations are likely to resurface. In this case, envy might arise in the subject and cause him/her to jeopardize the chances of the person standing before him/her. The role of recruiter requires the ability to be considerate of the others, to help and encourage them to fulfill their talents in a healthy environment. This is possible only if the persons have been able, through inner work, to acknowledge and accept their limitations, failures, and deficiencies.

Envy and mentoring

This ability is also essential in the case of mentoring: in order to guide and support somebody in their professional development and play the role of mentor, one must be able not to feel threatened by this development. Here again, this is only possible if those in the mentoring role are able to refrain from comparing themselves with the other, or at least not to let this comparison affect them negatively, so that they can behave supportively and considerately towards the other.

Yet, very often, the more a mentoree's skills grow, the more similar/close he/she becomes to his/her mentor, and the more likely envy is to develop:

> The mentor may envy the fresh opportunities that the protégé's new abilities and youth allow, in addition to resenting the protégé's wish to become independent. The mentor may feel disappointed and angry at what he considers the protégé's lack of gratitude. Mentors are particularly likely to feel resentful if they are stuck themselves, if they see little opportunity for their own advancement. It looks to them as if they have simply prepared someone to displace them. Some mentors may begin to make more demands on their protégés while insisting they are not ready to go out on their own. Some may even take steps to block their protégés from leaving or finding new positions elsewhere.[13]

There is a story in the Bible that provides food for thought about the emergence of envy in mentoring relationships.[14] In the biblical account, Joshua was Moses' beloved disciple; Moses had prepared him to take over as political and military leader of the people of Israel. When the time of Moses' death approached, God instructed him to transfer the mantle of leadership to Joshua. Moses accepted this request but begged God to let him live, albeit with a reversal of his role: "Let me be [Joshua's] disciple." God granted him his request. However, it soon became clear that "even the great Moses, about whom it was said in the Bible that he was the humblest man on earth, couldn't handle the new situation in which the mentor has been supplanted by his pupil in both honor and access to divine wisdom".[15] Realizing that his new position as disciple was unbearable to him and caused him to envy Joshua, Moses chose to renounce this role and let himself die: "Rather a hundred deaths than a single pang of envy."

Career management and individuals' respective places

Career management practices, and in particular the way promotion processes are conducted, provide other opportunities to modify individuals' respective places and consequently to trigger envy among employees. A few examples of this have been presented.

Thus, the professor who hears that his colleague has obtained a post in a more prestigious university feels envious. In the Hong Kong bank, the promotion assessment process, which takes place every two years, is a period during which envy arises among some of the employees who have not been promoted. In Noemie's case, it is hardly surprising that the onset of her depression coincided with the time when her colleague, whom she perceived as her equal, was promoted to the post of team manager while she was not. The envy she then feels towards her colleague is so strong as to become destructive, particularly to herself.

A promotion that opens a gap between individuals

In the cases described above, envy arises because, when one person is promoted and not the other, a gap opens between two comparable people and modifies their respective places. A study has shown that the promotion of one of the partners to a position of formal authority over the other was one of the primary causes of workplace friendship deterioration.[16] The accounts given by the people who were interviewed show that change in status is difficult to accept for people who are not promoted. The deterioration of relationships between individuals could be interpreted as a manifestation of envy. People, who, because they are promoted, change places, suddenly stand apart. They position themselves in a place that creates a gulf between the others and themselves. The person who has not been promoted is suddenly brought face to face with his/her own limitations.

It is important to note, however, that a promotion does not systematically trigger envy. Two factors seem to play a decisive role: high promotion expectations, and a high level of perceived similarity between the rejected individual and the promoted individual that would enhance workplace envy.[17] "Deprivation experienced from being rejected for promotion when expectations were high would result in a mild negative reaction (disappointment), but [. . .] this reaction would be exacerbated into envy when perceived similarity was high."[18]

The disastrous effects of a poorly handled promotion

The examples described above show that the feelings of envy triggered by a promotion can lead to a variety of reactions:

- In the first case, the professor manages to overcome his envy by detaching himself from his friend and by being able to look at him from a healthy perspective;
- In the second case, the employees who have not been promoted and feel envious of those who have strive to improve their performance so as to have a better chance of being promoted the next time;
- In the third case, Noemie, whose feelings of envy have their roots in a pathological process, sinks into depression.

Envy can also lead to extreme violence against the envied; Shakespeare's famous play *Othello* provides a superb example of how a badly handled promotion can lead to envy, with disastrous consequences.

Case 22: **A mishandled promotion that has left its mark over the centuries**[19]

Othello is known to be a great military general serving in the Venetian army and secretly married to the beautiful Desdemona, the daughter of a Venetian senator. Othello, on the eve of going to war against the Turks, must choose someone as his lieutenant.

Iago is Othello's ensign (a job also known as an ancient or standard-bearer). Counting on Othello's trust in him, Iago hopes that he will be promoted to the post of lieutenant. However, Othello chooses Cassio, a young and inexperienced soldier. Iago cannot bear the fact that Othello overlooked him in favor of Cassio and, filled with hatred and envy, starts conspiring against Cassio and Othello, using Othello's trust in him to manipulate him. Manipulating Cassio into discrediting himself, Iago succeeds in getting Othello to dismiss Cassio from the post of lieutenant and to put him in Cassio's place. But Iago wants more revenge and still hates Othello. He manipulates Othello into believing that his wife, Desdemona, is having an affair with Cassio. His malicious plans end up in a bloodbath: Othello kills his wife and, realizing her innocence, kills himself. By the end of the play, much of the Venetian military leadership is in ruins.

Although Shakespeare's dramatic play was set in Venice four centuries ago, it provides a typical illustration of how a promotion can lead to envy. Iago has proved his worthiness to Othello, but Cassio is chosen because he is an "arithmetician", a "scholar" and is better educated than Iago.[20] In a modern organization also, a person from the outside may be chosen for a position because he or she has higher qualifications than another person who is already employed in the organization and aspires to the same position.

Another, very modern, aspect of this play lies in the fact that Othello's selection of Cassio as his lieutenant was done publicly, which contributes all the more to the humiliation felt by Iago that the three "great ones of the city" had supported him in his application to Othello. His failure is therefore public, and is witnessed by all the noblemen of the city. In a similar way, when, during a promotion process in an organization, employees compete for particularly prestigious positions that are reserved for the employees with the "highest potential", the failure of those who are not promoted is all the more humiliating and painful as it takes place publicly. This is bound to reinforce envy in them.

This case shows that a poorly managed promotion can have serious consequences if it generates envy. The passed-over employee may seek revenge, in a more or less subtle way: by spreading rumors about their rival, by putting obstacles in the way of the person who has been promoted, by intentionally keeping important information from the latter, which necessarily impacts negatively on the quality of the work performed.

An environment that either fosters envy or keeps it in check

The feelings of envy related to the promotion of a person can in some cases be so strong that the envious subjects might do everything in their power to jeopardize their colleague's promotion. Thus, in the New Zealand university mentioned earlier, an evaluation committee must decide whether a gifted young lecturer should be given tenure or not. Some influential members of the committee are envious of the young woman's qualities but disguise their feelings, pretending that their decision to reject her application was made objectively.

An experimental study has shown that the envious subjects surveyed made decisions against people they envied, but only did so if they thought or knew that those decisions could not be attributed to them. If, on the other hand, there was any chance that their decisions could be made public, they tended to side in favor of the people they envied and supported the latter more than the non-envious people did. This could be interpreted as a social defense mechanism enabling individuals to hide envy.[21]

In Shakespeare's play, Iago manipulates Othello, carries out his plot for revenge undetected, and manages to hide the feelings of envy he experiences when he is passed over in favor of Cassio. In the case of the evaluation committee, the envious members pretend that the decision was made in compliance with standard rules and procedures. They take advantage of the ambiguity of the evaluation criteria to interpret them in a way that suits them, and in doing so make a perfectly unfair but "justifiable" decision. The aggressiveness and hostility caused by envy here are disguised under the pretense of objectivity, which makes it impossible to detect the role played by the envious persons: the decision appears to have emanated from the group.

This example draws attention to a type of environment that is more conducive to envy: in the Hong Kong bank, the envious individuals have no influence on the decision to promote such and such an employee, whereas the promotion and tenure procedures of the university allow the envious subjects enough leeway to block their colleague's promotion.

The dangers of evaluation "by peers"

This case illustrates certain risks associated with systems whereby "peers" evaluate each other and manage each other's careers: These practices are common in certain professional environments (and particularly in universities) and are based on the postulate that only "peers" are able to evaluate the quality of the work performed by their colleagues and to assess their capacity to progress. Some sociologists have highlighted that practices such as bargaining arrangements, lobbying, and political factors impacted on such evaluation processes,[22] but here, just as in the analyses of resistance to change, by placing too much emphasis on these power-related issues, one might omit to mention the impact that other more psychological aspects related to the emotions and insecurities of people involved might also have on these evaluation processes. Indeed, from a psychological perspective, placing employees in a position to evaluate their "peers" is not without risk; emotions such as envy might affect the judgment of people who make decisions concerning their colleagues' careers. The case of the young lecturer discussed above is a typical example of such a scenario. Let us bear in mind that individuals tend to envy people with whom they feel "similar" or comparable.

An unbearable dependency

The feelings of envy experienced by subjects are rooted in the fantasy that what the other possesses should rightfully be theirs.[23] Envious individuals feel deprived at the very sight of what the people they envy possess and seem to enjoy; and seeing this pleasure in the others causes the envious unbearable suffering. Envy is often associated with feelings of intense frustration.[24]

In this process, the envious individual feels linked to the envied by an invisible thread: what one possesses, one possesses at the expense of the other. The only object capable of satisfying the envious is the one that the other possesses; which explains the envious' desire to either acquire it for him/herself or deprive the envied of it. As René Girard has shown, it is not the rarity of the object the envied possesses that makes it desirable to the envious: the relationship between the envious and the envied existed before the latter acquired the object; what makes the object desirable to the envious is the fact that the other, to whom he/she is connected, possesses and desires it, which implies that the envious is deprived of it. Beneath envy lies a strong dependence of the envious on the envied.

According to psychoanalyst Melanie Klein, the first experiences of envy occur at a time in very early childhood when infants still depend entirely on their mothers for survival, and do not yet experience themselves as separate from their mothers.[25] According to Melanie Klein, infants sometimes perceive the maternal breast as the bad object that keeps for itself the milk, the love, and the care associated with the good breast, as the object that deprives them of this satisfaction. They might then start hating and envying this parsimonious breast and wish, fanstasmatically, to destroy it so as to prevent an other from possessing and enjoying it. In this "primitive" envy, an infant's destructive desires are so intense that he/she is prepared, fantasmatically, to destroy the breast on which his/her very survival depends. It is not self-preservation that the infant seeks here but the destruction of the object of envy. In this description, the strong initial dependence of the envious on the envied seems to be an essential condition of the emergence of envy.

Similarly, in organizations, envy often arises when the dependence between several individuals (or services) intensifies.

Depending on the same resources

Thus, at times when organizational resources are being allocated, envy is likely to emerge. The term resource is used in a wide sense here. In an organizational environment, they can be financial resources (budget), resources related to the organization's activities (clients, information, employment, or means), or symbolic resources (titles and distinctions). Any resource allocation process can give rise to feelings of frustration and, as a result, envy.

Destroying the nourishing breast

In the introduction to this book, I mentioned the example of the consulting firm founded by four friends. While the four friends were working together to organize themselves as a group (define the positioning and name of the firm, the legal status of the partners, and their communication strategy), there were no tensions between them. The difficulties arose when the firm started getting contracts and missions had to be allocated. The four consultants had different skills in complementary fields of consulting and the missions were distributed on this basis and in such a way as to match skills to demand. But this arrangement seems to have generated strong feelings of frustration and envy in Peter: he considered contracts as resources and he needed to make sure that the other members did not get more contracts than he did. Fantasmatically, he feared that the others would take the "good breast" away from him. His fears, though ungrounded, were no less intense. His reactions might have had their roots in his personal history.

What is interesting here is that Peter started experiencing feelings of envy the moment the question of resource allocation was raised, and resources were abundant. But Peter would rather destroy the organization than work under these conditions. If we examine his reaction from the perspective of Melanie Klein's theory, it seems that Peter chose to destroy the breast he depended on – because it was source of intense frustration – rather than let anyone else feed on it.

Sharing rarified resources

The case above shows that envy often has its roots in the imaginary; indeed, in this example, there is no shortage of resources. However, in some cases, individuals have to share scarce, or diminishing, resources. Such conditions foster the fantasy that what one obtains is taken from another: I don't have something because an other has it. The scarcer the resources appear to be, the stronger the interdependence between individuals (or services or teams) seems to get: one cannot ignore the fact that others are also waiting for the resources to be allocated. In an environment where resources are scarce or limited, envy is more than likely to increase.

Another, admittedly extreme, example is provided by Anne-Lise Stern,[26] a survivor of a German concentration camp.

Case 23: Killing for a chunk of bread
In Anne-Lise Stern's account of her ordeal, it appears that it was the constant, piercing hunger that caused the most unbearable suffering; this was confirmed by other former prisoners such as Primo Levi or Jorge Semprun. She describes how, driven by suffering, she starts feeling envious of other prisoners: she is prepared to annihilate, kill a woman who has a chunk of bread, a resource she wants to obtain whatever the cost.

This is a good illustration of the primitive envy that Melanie Klein describes: envy of the maternal breast that may or may not provide food and care for the infant. The extreme conditions of deprivation that prevailed in the camps awakened long buried and primitive feelings related to survival, and generated feelings of envy in the prisoner.

I mentioned earlier the case of the university, in which the catering and maintenance departments decided not to cooperate with the training department; indeed, the members of these departments felt envious of the lecturers because they were not affected by a decision of outsourcing. It would be interesting to know how the management justified their decision. Indeed, my experience in the field of reorganization has shown me that when a decision to close down certain departments or eliminate certain jobs is justified by the wish to save or develop other departments of the organization, there is a high probability that envy will emerge; indeed, such a justification validates the illusion that what the others have, the others are deprived of.

More generally, it is possible to identify the times, in all organizations, when resources are distributed and when as a result envy might emerge: the budget allocation period in most organizations, the times when the top managers of a corporation decide on the number of posts to be allocated to each department, when resources such as offices, company cars, secretarial support, travel money are allocated, etc.

Depending on someone else's skills

There are also instances when, at work, an individual can strongly depend on the skills of another person, skills which the individual him/herself does not possess. Fantasmatically speaking, this configuration is very similar to the situation of "primitive envy" described by Melanie Klein.

Dependence in a team

The case below provides a good illustration of this type of workplace envy.

Case 24: The enraged tutor[27]

Karine, a Masters student in management, has until now obtained good marks and been considered a serious student. She also achieved good assessment results during her on-the-job training periods.

At the end of the Masters year, she does her practical training in a firm called Tracta, at the external communication department managed by Anne. Karine's mission, defined during the recruitment interview, is to participate in a study aimed at evaluating the impact of an information letter submitted by Tracta to its clients and partners. It is the first time Anne is put in charge of a study. This study is divided into several phases. The answers are coded and analyzed using SPSS (Statistical Package for the Social Sciences) data analysis software Karine has used during her training at the university, which owns an SPSS license. Her tutor, Anne, is unwilling to invest in this expensive technology but insists that the data be processed with this software, and asks Karine, when she is recruited for the course, to work with the version owned by the university.

Anne relies entirely on Karine and on another trainee whom she recruits one month later and who has a specialized postgraduate degree (Anne had initially considered recruiting a vocational training school student). Although the second trainee was, at first, supposed to assist Karine, Anne decides to give each trainee the same task, which places them in a position to compete with each other.

The study takes longer than anticipated; the deadline seems to be too short. The training period was supposed to take place between mid-April and June, but Anne asks Karine to stay until the end of July so that she can complete the study. Karine accepts the request, although the relations between herself and her tutor are growing tense. She talks of "harassment" from her tutor.

When Karine eventually completes the training period and leaves the firm, she has not yet written the conclusion of the study because the data collection was not performed in time and the analysis of this data has only just been completed. Anne puts pressure on Karine to complete the report even though the official training period is over, and threatens not to pay her and not to validate her training, which would result in Karine not obtaining her Masters Degree. No longer able to tolerate her tutor's threats, Karine refuses. At the end of August, Anne sends a letter to the university in which she belittles the work performed by the student, compares her unfavorably with the other trainee, and asks that her training not be validated.

Can Karine really be considered as lacking professional competence? The answer is, without hesitation, no! It was her tutor herself who insisted on Karine staying longer in the firm; thanks to her methodological skills and her knowledge of the software, she made a precious contribution. Also, Anne's insistence that Karine herself write the conclusion of the study tends to show that Anne considers the student as competent (and even indispensable). Furthermore, Karine is a serious student and her other practical training periods have been successful. In this context, how can one explain the conflictual nature of the relationship between tutor and trainee?

In this case, it is important to take into account the dependence of the tutor on her trainee and its potential consequences. Indeed, as mentioned above, Anne depends on Karine: the latter alone has access to and is capable of using the data analysis software. From the start, her relationship with Karine is strange: Anne is her tutor and therefore her direct superior but she recruits Karine because of her skills; skills she admits she does not possess herself. This makes her dependent on the student. Furthermore, the project has important implications for her future (the results of the study will determine whether or not she is useful; indeed the study is aimed at evaluating the impact of an information letter which the department she is in charge of has produced). Her dependence on Karine is made clear by the fact that she openly asks Karine to postpone her departure from Tracta and puts pressure on the trainee to write the conclusions of the report.

Because she cannot bear being dependent on Karine, Anne becomes aggressive towards her. She closely monitors Karine's working hours, constantly controls her work, and systematically criticizes it. She never acknowledges the trainee's qualities (but has to ask her to postpone her departure, which implicitly shows that she is happy with Karine's work), as this would require that she accept her own limitations. What is remarkable is the rage and destructive energy she displays when she realizes that she will not manage to coerce Karine into completing the report. The letter she sends to the university is very accusatory: she only mentions Karine's "deficiencies". What she wants is to prevent Karine from graduating.

It must also be noted that Anne systematically places Karine and the other trainee in competing positions. Although she was supposed to recruit a vocational training school student to assist Karine, Anne decides to recruit a student with a specialized postgraduate degree, one who is constantly reflected in Karine's mirror. Instead of encouraging them to collaborate, she gives both trainees the same tasks so that she can compare their performance. In the letter she sends to the university, she explicitly compares Karine with the other trainee ("her colleague has been up to the challenge") and emphasizes the success of the one and failure of the other. The destructive and aggressive force that takes hold of her, as well as her dependence on Karine's skills, lead us to believe that envy is at the origin of her behavior. This hypothesis is all the more plausible since Anne intentionally places Karine in a position that could have caused the latter to experience feelings of envy and rivalry towards the other trainee. Anne is very aware of the mirror relationship that develops between Karine and herself, and so tries to force her into a position where she will also be confronted with her own limitations. All these processes probably occur unconsciously. As for Karine, she feels attacked and placed in an ambiguous position that she cannot understand: on the one hand, her tutor cannot do without her, and on the other the latter systematically belittles her work and professional abilities. She experiences the events with complete disbelief and shock.

Naturally these hypotheses would need to be validated clinically, which has not been the case here. However, they present the merit of linking elements that are, a priori, contradictory or extreme. They help us to understand a situation that had serious consequences from a relational point of view, even though the work performed by the student in question was satisfactory. They also draw our attention to a type of situation, often encountered in the workplace, in which a person strongly depends on another employee who possesses skills he or she does not possess.

Depending on a consultant

There are also cases when consultants may be envied by the very people or teams they are supposed to help.[28] They may be attacked precisely because they possess skills or qualities on which the people they have come to help depend. This phenomenon is very similar to what psychoanalysts, following Melanie Klein, have called "negative therapeutic reactions".[29] This term refers to the frequent observation, during psychotherapeutic processes, that a period of improvement can be followed by a period of deterioration of the patient's state, as if the patient unconsciously resists recovery. At this stage, it is not uncommon for the patient to criticize the analyst, to systematically reject his/her interpretations, and to attempt to destabilize him/her. There are different possible causes for this phenomenon, such as the difficulty in coming to terms with what has been discovered through the therapy. Psychoanalysts consider that one frequent cause of this phenomenon is the development of envy in the patient's relationship with the analyst: getting better requires that patients recognize and accept the fact that they depend on the analyst, accept the "good things" that the latter may contribute, and possibly even feel gratitude towards him, which an envious person finds it impossible to do. Patients may also unconsciously deny the analyst the pleasure that their recovery might bring him/her. This is a typical case of envy in which people can put themselves in danger so as to deprive the other of a supposed pleasure.

When providing consulting services to an organization, one should therefore be aware of this phenomenon. When consultants place too much emphasis on their wish to help and in so doing draw attention to the fact that the people they help might have grown dependent on them, they might, paradoxically, generate reactions of envy that will hinder the resolution of the problem they were hired to solve.

Remaining vigilant

I have now identified certain types of situations that may trigger or accentuate envy in the workplace. Most organizations are likely to encounter such situations. Thus, promoting an employee, recruiting a new employee or trainee, placing two complementary people side by side in the same team, distributing resources, allocating budgets are all management tasks that are performed frequently. As for organizational change, though it does not occur as frequently and is not as "ordinary" as other tasks, it is nonetheless a process that takes place, more or less "smoothly" or on the contrary radically, in all organizations at some time or another.

All these situations take on new meaning when examined through the lenses of envy. Indeed, they are all situations that can trigger or reinforce this emotion. They therefore call for vigilance on the part of leaders and managers, who play a major role in these processes. As mentioned in Chapter 2, the existence of envy is an unavoidable aspect of social interaction, but it can in some cases become extremely destructive. It can turn into a noxious poison that is all the more dangerous that it is often undetected. Unfortunately, envy is often allowed to grow out of control in organizations that are not aware or do not acknowledge that certain situations are conducive to envy. Being able to identify such situations and knowing that they can have such an impact helps in managing them with more attention and vigilance.

I have grouped these situations into two categories, by showing that envy could emerge, firstly, when the respective places of individuals within the organization are changed or interchanged, and secondly, when the members of a team, a service, or an organization become overly interdependent.

Admittedly, this typology has limitations: the envy that occurs in the first type of situation might also be related to factors that prevail in the second type of situation. For example, when a firm undergoes reorganization, not only are the respective places of individuals changed, but the resources are also distributed differently, which accentuates the perceived dependence of some individuals or departments on others. The two scenarios are not exclusive of each other; on the contrary. The primary merit of this typology is to draw attention to two types of contextual factors that can trigger envy in organizations. If a situation combines the two types of factors, the chances are even higher that envy will arise and be active in the organization.

7
Healthier Organizations

We have reached a point in our discussion where we can no longer deny the existence of envy in the workplace. We are now able to spot it, hidden behind many different symptoms, organizational problems, and dysfunctions. We know why it develops in workplace settings, what forms it takes and what consequences it can have. We also know that certain types of situations are particularly conducive to triggering it.

But it is one thing to recognize its more or less active presence, it is quite another to know what to do about it, how to manage it, and whether we should take it into account.

The worst scenario: letting envy take control

Envy is inherent to life in society. Its presence in the workplace, as in any social group, is "normal". Anthropology has shown us that many traditional social systems are founded on the postulate, which must not be revealed, that envy can destroy the group and that one must therefore prevent it from awakening and growing. The functioning of the system is based on the recognition that envy exists and on the prevention of its development, but this knowledge must remain concealed. It is on this condition that the system survives.

This is not what happens in contemporary organizations. On the contrary, it seems that in a number of them, the human resources management policy is based on a profound knowledge of the mechanisms of envy, and that instead of striving to minimize its effects, the managers make it the mainspring of their motivational practices.

146

Thus, some systems allow envy to steer the ship and to become a central component of their functioning, at the risk of letting it have destructive consequences. The paradox of these systems is that, although they exploit envy as the basis of many management practices, they never mention its existence and do everything they can to conceal it. Thus, behind the rhetoric that promotes the autonomy of employees hides the fact that organizations often instill motivation in their employees by encouraging imitation and permanent comparison between them. Similarly, some organizations adopt "teamwork" as their official motto, but in reality push employees to compete against one another, which makes it impossible for them to truly collaborate. In such situations, the feelings of envy generated by the system can become extremely violent and turn against the organization – by causing a waste of human resources (Punchy) – or against the employee, when the latter's psychological make-up makes him or her prone to being enslaved by this type of functioning (Noemie).

My position is clear: organizations that adopt management and motivational practices that rest on the exploitation of envy play a dangerous and unhealthy game. Such practices mobilize the most infantile part of individuals' egos by exploiting their extreme dependence on evaluation and on the Other's recognition, and their difficulty to detach themselves from an "other" reflected in their mirror. When envy is allowed to fester in an organization, it hinders relational fluidity and mobilizes so much of individuals' psychic energy that they are caused to neglect aspects, such as creativity or collaboration, which are essential to the survival of the organization. One of the main managerial challenges related to envy is to develop human resource management systems that prevent envy from having destructive consequences on the organization and to be aware of the types of situations that may trigger envy.

There is no miracle recipe to achieve this. I have discussed the inefficiency of the solution that would involve trying to eradicate envy by developing an organizational structure based on an egalitarian principle that would rule every single aspect of life. Indeed, such systems would, first of all, have disastrous consequences in terms of innovation, productivity, and of capacity to progress, because of the fear of being envied; and secondly, they would fail to prevent the development of envy. On the contrary, the second aspect would be facilitated because the slightest differences would then take on unbearable proportions and would lead to latent envy.

Each organization has its own characteristics and one must approach the problem of envy by taking into account these specificities. A few guidelines can help to facilitate this process.

Limiting mimetic processes

First of all, one must strive to prevent or limit mimetic processes.

One possible means of doing so is to create and maintain differences between the members of teams, and in so doing promote diversity within the latter. One can achieve diversity in a team by ensuring that it is composed of people of both genders, different nationalities and social origins, different ages, experiences, or education. The more differences there are between individuals, the more difficult it is to compare oneself to others, and the less likely it is that only one single model will be perceived as desirable.

This can help managers beware situations in which individuals may be kept in each other's mirrors, be too strongly dependent on, or permanently face each other. Indeed, these are all situations in which envy is likely to develop and fester. Thus, in the case of the "enraged tutor", if the director had been aware of the latent feelings of envy that existed in Anne and Karine's relationship, he could have taken measures to "separate" the two women. For example, he could have decided to place Karine in his charge and to meet, on a regular basis, with Anne and the trainee to determine the progress of the project. Instead, he allowed a very unhealthy relationship to fester. In the case of Fanny and Cecilia, the management team has made the mistake of recruiting two students from the same cohort and with very similar profiles, and of appointing them to similar posts, causing them to work face to face with each other. The reorganization of the different departments helps to physically separate the two trainees. Generally speaking, promoting job autonomy, by minimizing opportunities for comparison, reduces the probabilities of envy developing.[1]

Limiting mimetic processes necessitates that certain separations be maintained in organizations, even at the risk of running counter to some current management trends. In an era when flexibility, interchangeability, flat hierarchical structures, versatility, and so on are advocated, we recommend on the contrary that certain boundaries and frontiers be maintained in order to clearly differentiate individuals' places, and thus avoid placing them in positions where they may compete with one another. In a totally open system in which places are interchangeable, processes of mimetic contagion are almost unavoidable, making it difficult to prevent the development of envy. Instead of remaining confined to one part of the system, envy is then highly likely to spread to and contaminate the system as a whole.

Avoiding getting stuck in failure and frustration

Being able to bounce back

The problem with envy in the workplace is not so much that it is there in the first place, but that it is often allowed to fester and that it is not converted into more positive energy. In an interview, a young e-commerce entrepreneur explained:

> A friend of mine started an eBay business two years ago. When I saw that the business was doing well and that he was earning good money, I felt envious and I belittled him. I used to say to our common friends: "It's not gonna go far; it's not gonna work." I reassured myself thinking: "He's spending a lot of time in a worthless business that's bound to fail." But as it was going from strength to strength, I started being interested in it and telling myself that maybe I could also get into it and do what he'd done. So I looked at the possibility and I made the jump. I wasn't envious anymore because I saw how fascinating the whole thing was and I realized that I could do something interesting. We even worked together.

This case shows that envy can be transformed and overcome, but the envious must first recognize it to be able to convert the negative energy into positive energy, and progress.

In the case of the Hong Kong bank, some of the employees who were not promoted did feel envy, but their feelings did not grow out of proportion. On the contrary, the envious individuals were those who, a few months after being rejected for promotion, achieved the highest performance results. They perceived their failure as temporary and the system allowed them to convert their feelings of envy into a motivation to progress.

Unfortunately, as noted earlier, not all organizational systems allow for such transformations. In some systems, members are kept under the impression that the only path to career development is the *royal path*, the latter simultaneously becoming the only truly valued (and therefore desirable) path, reserved to a very small number of people. In such environments, failing to climb the "royal" ladder can damage an individual's sense of self-worth, and if other career paths are not valued by the organization, individuals, then, cannot focus their attention on models that might be more suitable and accessible to them. In such situations, frustration is bound to increase and turn into envy. And as the latter develops it is likely to result in aggressive behavior towards the system or the people who succeed, long-term demotivation, or a disengagement from the system. Systems that consider only one type of path as valuable do not respect the other possible alternative routes that one could choose in relation to one's profession, and in so doing make this "one best way" almost inaccessible to most. Systems like these have a high probability of contracting the contagious disease of envy. This is why it is essential that management systems be designed in such a way as to accept and value plurality and diversity in individuals' professional paths (and origins), so as to prevent frustration from developing and people from getting bogged down in envy.

Turning failures into learning opportunities

Envy takes root and festers in individuals who cannot rid themselves of their feelings of inferiority, feelings which in general are kept untold. As I noted in the introduction, envy can be perceived as the negative side of a world that values success above all else. Envy is associated with failure, inferiority, and difficulties in achieving what we desire. From an organizational perspective, the challenge therefore consists in allowing individuals to overcome situations that have caused them to doubt their own competence and abilities. How is an employee's failure to be promoted dealt with by the organization? How does the group as a whole manage situations that are likely to make some employees feel insecure – for example, during a reorganization process? Is failure stigmatized or, on the contrary, accepted and talked about as an acceptable experience? Does the organization provide the employees with resources to help them overcome these difficulties? What kind of help, support, and guidance are the employees offered? A suitable career development plan, for example, can play an essential role in helping an employee rid him/herself of a feeling of inferiority and self-doubt and feel capable of progressing.

At Google, where teamwork and innovation are highly valued, the team members' failures are celebrated: because the members spend all their energy innovating and experimenting with new solutions, they are bound to fail every now and then; but failure must not detract them from their desire to try again. In this case, failure is examined, taking into account the initial risk taken by the employees and the fact that they attempted something new and unknown; failure is not viewed only in terms of its negative effects. There is, in this organization, a true desire not to stigmatize failure and not to let it endanger employees' sense of self-worth, but rather to welcome initiative. How many organizations can claim to be this coherent and consistent in the ways they encourage creativity in their employees?

Choosing the right managers

The manager can play an important role in the genesis of envy, and symmetrically in preventing it from taking root and becoming toxic. In many of the cases of extreme envy discussed in this book, the manager seems to be an aggravating factor and can even be the one that sows the seed of envy; for example, in the cases of Punchy, the Business School, Tracta, the university evaluation committee, the envious recruiter, and the airport.

Managers can play a relatively inactive – but nonetheless significant – role in the development of envy by failing to see that certain situations can foster it. Thus, in the case of Fanny and Cecilia, the manager does not seem to be aware of the tensions that arise between the two trainees and of the risks of envy entailed in placing two people with very similar profiles side by side. Similarly, Othello is oblivious to the fact that Iago feels envious when Cassio is promoted to the position of lieutenant. Othello naively believes that as far as Iago is concerned nothing has changed, whereas in fact a deep chasm has opened between them: his hope to be promoted has been betrayed, he has lost his reputation, and he feels ashamed and betrayed.

Othello keeps Iago in his team and continues to trust him. His blindness will have disastrous consequences.[2]

In extreme cases, managers can play a much more active and destructive role: they may actively strive to foster and exacerbate the feelings of envy that exist between employees, as in the cases of Punchy and the Business School; or they may themselves be envious of certain collaborators and take advantage of their position of power to attack them, as in the cases of Tracta and of the evaluation committee.

From envy to harassment

In these extreme cases, the managers have not been able to engage in the inner reflection that would have enabled them to acknowledge and come to terms with their own deficiencies. By trying to exacerbate envy between team members, they seek to ascend to a position of omnipotence, which enables them to repress their doubts about themselves and their awareness of their own limitations. By directly attacking colleagues they envy, they can enact their desire to harm and destroy those who have forced them to confront their own shortcomings and have caused them narcissistic suffering. This is, incidentally, how psychoanalysts explain harassing behavior at work. Harassers get fixated on a characteristic in one of their colleagues, and this causes them unbearable pain because its existence in the other reminds them of its absence in themselves;[3] hence their desire to destroy the other at all costs, to annihilate what makes the other different and superior in their eyes. Their attacks aim to eliminate those differences, and more generally, that "extra" quality or object that the other possesses. In this perspective, harassment is the consequence of strong and primitive envy that causes the envious person to want to destroy the object of envy. This is in keeping with the research on psychological harassment, which shows that victims of harassment are psychologically annihilated and feel they have lost all their vitality and self-confidence.

A constructive manager

Whether managers are oblivious or indifferent to the feelings of envy that potentially plague their teams, or are actively promoting their development, and even taking advantage of their position of power to harass colleagues they envy, they do play a central role. It is therefore essential that they be warned of its potential impact on the genesis of envy.

A few recommendations can be made to managers who wish to avoid reinforcing envy in their teams:

- Give all the employees for whom they are responsible the feeling that they are respected, that their work is appreciated and rewarded fairly;
- Avoid triggering the mechanisms of comparison. This implies that they themselves refrain from comparing their employees with one another. They must, on the contrary, try to acknowledge the specificity of the activities and tasks performed by each individual, and in so doing appreciate the specific skills each employee offers. They should also provide personalized feedback on a regular basis;
- Ensure that each employee has his/her own place and feels secure in it;
- Avoid belittling some members of the team by overly glorifying others;
- Prevent feelings of inferiority from festering, for example by reassuring employees who have failed in a task that this failure or difficulty had nothing to do with shortcomings or limitations in themselves that cannot be rectified, and by helping them move on and regain a positive state of mind.

Managers who work to minimize feelings of inferiority and bitterness, who keep comparison between individuals to a minimum and avoid making the comparison public, increase their chances of preventing envy from infecting the team. What is essential here is the managers' ability to establish respectful relationships with their employees so as to preserve the latter's sense of self-worth.[4]

Case 25: Competition and collaboration[5]
One employee of a large department store group in France describes his experience as follows: *"For a week there was a sales contest in all the stores of the group nationwide: those who at the end of each day had achieved the highest sales results were rewarded with a bottle of champagne. But the director of the store where I work decided that every morning of that week, the whole staff would be offered breakfast: whether or not you won the contest, you were given tea or coffee and croissants when you got to work in the morning. That meant that we were all part of the same team and that each member was thanked*

for his or her contribution to the collective effort. So, if you didn't win the bottle of champagne, it was no big deal: the bottle was a little extra but in any case, they thanked you by offering you breakfast." Let us compare this case to that of Punchy: (a) the contest only lasts for a week and the competition between the employees is not permanent; and (b) the director of the store ensures that each employee is recognized as a member of the team whose efforts must also be rewarded. This case shows that a contest does not necessarily generate envy: what matters is what is communicated concerning the "value" of each individual during the event.

A maturity that requires work

Being able, as a manager, to establish a constructive and supportive relationship with one's employees requires that he/she has worked on him/herself and has accepted his/her own limitations, doubts, and frustrations. This requires humility and self-compassion. Humility may be defined as:

> a non-defensive willingness to see the self accurately, including both strengths and weaknesses (. . .). Humility stems from an inner sense of security, a stable sense of worth and value that enables people to tolerate looking at their limitations without despair. (. . .) Humility is also linked with openness to new ideas and advice, an appreciation of the value of all things, and a desire for accurate self-evaluation that involves keeping one's abilities and accomplishments in perspective.[6]

As for self-compassion, it requires the ability to hold painful thoughts and feelings in balanced awareness, rather than over-identifying with them. It also requires that one be able to see one's experiences as being a common, connected aspect of human experience, rather than as isolating.[7]

Managers who are capable of limiting the development of envy in their work environment are the ones who can recognize their own feelings of envy when they emerge, and understand where they come from so as to be able to overcome them and not let them affect their behavior as managers. What is essential here is not so much to eliminate one's own envy, but rather to be able to identify and acknowledge it when it arises, to understand what triggers it, and to minimize its potentially destructive effects. It is the responsibility of organizations to choose managers who are mature enough psychologically and who have a balanced enough perspective on themselves to be able to prevent the development of envious behavior in their teams.

Being able to assert oneself as a subject in the organization

To overcome envy or to prevent it from affecting one's behavior, one must be able to refrain from engaging in a mimetic relationship with an other. This is what sociologist Helmut Schoeck meant when he wrote: "[. . .] the envious man will only be able to give his life value when he has elaborated a theory which, diverting his eyes from the children of fortune that potentially reinforce his envy, will channel his energy towards goals that are more accessible and better match his personality."[8] This requires that individuals be mature enough psychologically to gain perspective on the codes of success at work in the organization, without necessarily denying or rejecting them, and to relate to work in a manner that is respectful of themselves, of their abilities and desires. This position enables individuals to make professional choices according to the significance those choices have for themselves, to what they wish to contribute, and according to their own characteristics and qualities, experience, likes, and dislikes. To overcome envy, one must be able to refrain from reasoning in terms of superiority or inferiority to others, and from viewing the other or oneself as potentially omnipotent. This requires that the imaginary beliefs about oneself and the other be questioned. It also requires that individuals come to terms with their own limitations, deal with their ambivalent feelings, and clarify the implications of their professional choices in terms of losses and of opportunities. Envy projects individuals outside their own history, into a temporal space that does not belong to them; by making sense of their own choices and experiences, individuals can re-appropriate their own history and then fully recognize their place as autonomous subjects who heed their own desires.

Ability assessment, coaching, and self-worth

From a practical human resource management point of view, the question is whether the organization is willing to recognize this subject. The organization must be prepared to accept the fact that individuals have their own preferences and characteristics, and that individuals, as well as deciding upon their overall life choices, determine the professional choices they make. A personalized career development plan can serve as a means of helping an individual gain autonomy if it is undertaken as part of a carefully thought out professional project. It may enable employees to evaluate their own situation, to highlight the particular characteristics of their experience, and to think about their professional goals and desires.

As for coaching and personal development programs, which are becoming increasingly popular among certain categories of professionals, such as managers and business people for example, they can help individuals pay more attention to who they are and what they desire, and define professional and personal projects that are coherent with their wishes and personality. Unfortunately, many of these "coaching" programs have the opposite effects in that they reinforce the ego of the participants and validate their illusions of omnipotence and total control, thus maintaining them in the position of the infant facing the mirror, a position described extensively in this book.

A professional experience that makes sense

For individuals in the workplace to be able to position themselves as subjects, they must also have a full understanding of the framework within which they make their choices: the rules governing the evaluation of their work and their career development must be clear enough to enable the employees to define and position themselves in relation to those rules and thus to decide, in an informed way, which path to pursue. In the case of Punchy, it is almost impossible for the salespeople to position themselves as subjects, in that the framework constantly changes and the employees operate with no certainty. Their actions cannot be part of a well thought out, coherent plan, and the quasi impossibility of being promoted to higher positions (for obvious reasons here, very rare are those who are promoted to the posts of sales supervisor and store manager) is reinforced by the daily repetitiveness of the tasks; each day, the employees have to start all over again. They are separated from their past, they no longer have a history, and neither do their colleagues; the illusion that the other is one's double is validated.

In contrast, the university lecturer who is initially envious of a colleague who has found a better job can progressively look at his friend with enough perspective to attribute the gap that has opened between them to the fact that they each have their own characteristics and history. Rather than wishing for what his friend has obtained, he strives to understand what the differences between them mean. This is probably possible because the system in which he operates allows him to make sense of his own choices and to position them as part of the professional path he has pursued. He is allowed to re-appropriate his own history by engaging in self-reflection or in what Freud called "a working-through process",[9] in order to understand his feelings of envy and more generally his life choices. The main challenge, from the perspective of human resource management, is to ensure that the framework in which individuals operate and make choices is sufficiently coherent and evolutive to enable them to take ownership of their own history, without which they would be unable to position themselves as subjects.

Towards a "good enough" organization?

The primary responsibility of organizations is not so much to eradicate envy but to limit its potentially destructive effects. In order to meet this challenge, it is essential that, when they arise, the feelings of envy be allowed to be converted and used either to stimulate individuals to better themselves, as in the case of the Hong Kong bank, or as an opportunity for individuals to examine themselves, understand where their envy comes from, and rediscover the uniqueness of their professional history. This conversion, which prevents envy from festering in and poisoning the system, can only take place in what we shall call "a good enough organization" – as a variation on the concept of "good enough mother" introduced by British psychiatrist and psychoanalyst, Donald Winnicott. A "good enough organization" is one that:

- Limits individuals' anxiety about themselves;
- Maintains enough distance between its employees;
- Provides them with sufficient resources and distributes the latter on the basis of explicit, stable, and accepted rules;
- Does not exploit the narcissistic dimensions of weakened individuals to push them deeper and deeper into the system;
- Enables individuals to position themselves within a coherent professional framework;
- Avoids turning failures into dramas, and gives the employees the opportunity to try again.

Card 5   What can one do to prevent envy from growing out of proportion?

To prevent envy from gaining a foothold in a system, there are many things managers should beware of. Here are some recommendations that will help you.

Performance evaluation

In each activity, ensure that you use specific and clear performance measurement criteria. They are more difficult to implement and use, but they will enable you to take into account the specific skills associated with each function.

Be aware that asking for teamwork and at the same time placing emphasis on individual performance does not make sense:

- If a task requires teamwork, use criteria of measurement of the collective performance;
- Limit internal competition.

In many fields of activities, individuals' performance is difficult to measure. This is why:

- It is better not to evaluate at all than evaluate inaccurately;
- Avoid over-simplistic criteria;
- Perform qualitative evaluations, as much as is possible, with personalized feedback; they help the employee move forward.

For an evaluation to have any meaning for the employee/colleague, it is necessary to:

- Help him/her analyze and understand it;
- Avoid comparing him/her with others. Rather compare him/her to him/herself so as to reveal his/her accomplishments and areas that could be improved.

Your colleagues are people, not machines; they can, at times, face difficulties and as a result work less efficiently. Take this into account.

Rewards and incentives

Ensure that the reward rules are clear and known to all and that they take into account the nature of the employees' tasks.

Avoid systems that introduce artificial distinctions:

- A progressive incentive system is preferable: a bonus calculated individually and proportional to individual target achievements is preferable to a trip awarded to a few individuals. Avoid making clear distinctions between the "best", the "worst", and the others;
- Putting some employees "on stage" and rewarding them in "medal award ceremonies" or the like is not a good idea;
- Rather, use ceremonies and official events to celebrate, with all your colleagues, a collective success, or to encourage one another when you and your colleagues encounter difficulties.

Recruitment

Privilege diversity when recruiting.

Be vigilant when you recruit a new person: assess how the recruitment of this person will impact on the existing employees' positions:

- How will the balance in the team be affected?
- If you are recruiting a person who is particularly gifted in a particular area, be aware of the possible reactions of the other team members. Show that this person will be an asset to the team as a whole and that his/her contribution will benefit everyone;
- Continue showing your appreciation to the other members of the team at all times.

Be extremely vigilant when two people with very similar characteristics (gender, age, training, experience) must work together:

- If possible make a clear distinction between their functions;
- Give them different types of missions so as to make it more difficult to compare them with each other, but also to prevent them from comparing each other;

- In case of tension, separate them physically so that they do not have to face each other too often;
- Ensure that one does not depend on the other.

If you are the recruiter or mentor, be aware that the person you must recruit or mentor might awaken some fears in you:

- Do his/her skills and experience trigger frustration in you?
- If you feel envious, do the exercise described in Card 4.

Promotion and career management

Take measures to ensure that the people who have been promoted do not become the objects of envy. When a person is promoted, it is essential that he/she perform his/her new functions in a new team.

Limit feelings of frustration by:

- Defining career paths that are open and that take into consideration the skills of each individual. Of course you cannot be expected to define a different career path for every single individual, but avoid the "one best way" and the obstacles that come with it in terms of career;
- Define paths that provide opportunities to move forward. Moving up slowly but steadily is better than being stuck at the bottom of the ladder because the steps are too high.

Help your team members bounce back after a failure by:

- Developing a group culture that does not stigmatize failure: celebrate failures, talk about your own failures, etc.;
- Helping individuals analyze their experience, even if the result is disappointing, so that they can convert it into an opportunity to learn;
- Offering your colleagues the opportunity to try again or to attempt new projects;
- Recommending individual mentoring if necessary, after a failure.

Help the employees choose a professional path that makes sense to them by:

- Providing personalized feedback;
- Allowing the employees to attend personalized training courses that will help them reach their goals;
- Coaching – which can be one means of achieving this.

Do not let feelings of injustice grow; clearly define the rules on the basis of which promotion is granted. Apply these rules and only these rules.

If possible, ensure that the decision-makers are not too similar (i.e. have similar professional characteristics) to the employees applying for promotion:

- Ensure that those who make promotion decisions are more "neutral". Include people from the human resources board, an independent expert, etc.;
- In the case of evaluation "by peers", the only way of limiting envy-based discrimination is to ensure that the rules and criteria are clear and defined in advance, and that they are strictly complied with.

Distribution of resources: budget, clients, information, employment, etc.

- Clearly define the objectives that the available resources must help reach, and communicate these objectives to all parties.
- Define and communicate the allocation rules that will help reach this objective.
- You could also invite the different parties to participate in the definition of these rules.
- Strictly apply these rules. Play the transparency card.

Organizational change

Reassure all employees about their respective positions:

- Inform the employees, as soon as possible, about what posts they will have (or will not have) in the new structure;

- Clearly explain the rules on which the attribution of new posts was based;
- Predefine the rules aimed to promote equity; for example:
  - Rule of parity: if two organizations are to be merged, ensure if possible that the managerial posts are filled by employees from both organizations;
  - Rule of similarity: if two people have similar skills and functions, ensure that they are given similar career development opportunities in the new organization;
  - Sharing rule: if possible, the gains and losses associated with the reorganization should be clear to all and should be shared equally between the two organizations.

Be aware of the possible effects the change of positions of individuals might have on their relationships:

- If several people from the same department are going to carry on working together in the new organization, ensure if possible that their respective positions are not changed radically;
- If some individuals are promoted to better positions because of the reorganization, and others are not, try not to put them in the same team;
- If this is not possible, keep a close eye on them and separate them if envy arises.

Reassure the employees whose positions are going to change by:

- Helping them adapt to their new functions (training, tutoring, monitoring, etc.);
- Helping them view this change as part of their career development. Even if they experience this change as a move backwards, having to adapt forces them to find new resources within themselves;
- Showing that you appreciate their efforts, even if they are minimal.

Card 6   What can one do to avoid being the target of envy?[10]

We might, sometimes, be envied by others, which can be very unpleasant. Here are a few recommendations to avoid this type of situation.

Be a strong team player

- Anything that builds a sense of connection, conveying warmth, caring, and empathy, could help to defuse envy.
- Being accepted as a team player can thwart feelings of envy among one's teammates. For this purpose, one must show humility, share the successes with one's teammates, avoid going it alone, promote teamwork, and encourage your teammates to work together around common objectives.

Avoid putting yourself in the spotlight

- Do not give your colleagues too much information about yourself and your private life as this information might cause some to envy you or might be used by envious individuals;
- Avoid boasting about your achievements: being able to laugh at yourself, to admit that you too can experience difficulties, or that luck has sometimes favored you can defuse envy. This is not to say that you should use false modesty but that you should look at yourself from a realistic perspective.

Show appreciation for the person who envies you

- You could invite him/her to work with you on a common project;
- You could ask him/her for help in certain specific areas. This requires that you identify the areas in which the envious person's skills can be used and that you acknowledge and value these skills. By being willing to admit your own weaknesses and seeking the other's expertise, you show the latter that you are able to work toward an interpersonal balance and connection, and you avoid being seen as always in the high-status position.

Introduce processes of emotional regulation

- Coaching, or the services of a consultant, can be used for this purpose. They can help employees become aware of their feelings of envy, understand them, and in so doing minimize their destructive effects.

Be willing to distance yourself from the envious person

- You might sometimes become the object of envious attacks that might be difficult to thwart. In this case it might be a good idea to distance yourself, physically, from the envious person: by offering the person another post, or by assigning the latter missions that will enable him/her to work further away from you. You may also decide to move to a different position or different organization yourself.
- Some organizational systems, such as Punchy, are "sick": adversarial relationships and distrust are encouraged and envy is a direct consequence of these management systems. Ensure that you can identify them and leave them if you feel uncomfortable working in such conditions.

Conclusion
Envy and How We Relate with Others in the Workplace

Having reached the end of this book, I hope to have shed some light on a dark side of how some contemporary organizations work. There is no glory in envy: when it develops in an organization, it reveals that our behavior at work is conditioned by immature psychological processes. I have, in this book, put emphasis on the fact that organizations' management systems do play a role in either reinforcing or minimizing it. Some human resource management techniques, as we have seen, even seem to be based on the exploitation of human beings' propensity to fall back into infantile patterns such as those associated with envy, while at the same time dissimulating this dimension under a rhetoric of autonomy, excellence, emulation, etc.

An emotion that is likely to spread

One of the questions I would like to raise at the end of this analysis is the following: will this emotion arise even more frequently in organizations in future? The answer, unfortunately, is yes. Some of the management techniques and practices we have described in this book (comparison, evaluation, performance measurement tools, emphasis on competition, exploitation of mimetic processes, etc.) are here to stay. Indeed, they are used in an increasing number of organizations (private, public, cultural, etc.) and seem to have developed in response to a more general evolution, that of society. Some observers of western society warned, 20 years ago, against the impact of these evolutions[1] and predicted a generalized development of envy. I, in turn, am of the opinion that these management practices have become such an intrinsic part of modern organizational systems that the spread of envy will not be stopped anytime soon!

Yet, the management literature is silent on this subject, which seems paradoxical: envy is becoming more and more prevalent in organizations and yet is largely ignored by the theoretical literature. But the paradox is only superficial. Indeed, this lack of theoretical acknowledgement of envy contributes to the development of this emotion by dissimulating the processes at work in envy behind rhetoric about performance, excellence, and competition. This phenomenon is general and not limited to the field of management. Envy was given an important role in the literary works of the Antiquity (Aristotle), of the Renaissance (Ronsard, du Bellay), of the Baroque era (Shakespeare), and of the 17th and 18th centuries (La Fontaine, Pascal, Montaigne, Rousseau, Racine, Corneille). It is central in the works of many 19th century authors, such as Balzac, Stendhal, Zola, or Proust. They portrayed envy as affecting all circles, all social classes and professions, and as disrupting the destiny of individuals and relationships between people,[2] lurking beneath the warmest and most intimate friendships. In the 20th century, on the other hand, the topic disappeared from philosophical and literary works, and yet, according to the few sociologists who studied it, envy was spreading in direct relation to the development of capitalism.

Our hypothesis here is that envy is no longer just the result of life in society, but that it is the driving force behind it. The theoretical silence on the subject is directly related to this evolution: this force can only work if its presence at the heart of the system remains concealed. In contemporary organizations, the silence concerning envy allows it to remain a central component of them. It is this silence that I have sought to break because my experience has shown me that envy can have extremely destructive effects when it is repressed and concealed. The time has come to give it a name, to recognize it, and become aware of the serious effects it can have on a system in which it is allowed to fester.

"Relationship diseases"

The issue of envy in the workplace is related to a question that is fundamental to the survival of all organizations: that of how we relate to others. The development of envy has to do with what we could call "relationship diseases". When envy develops, a person's relationship with the other is damaged and is potentially destructive. But bonds between human beings are essential to an organization. Indeed organizations must manage to get different people to work together in order to be able to produce something that can only be produced by individuals as a group. Admittedly, standards and procedures contribute to this production, but they cannot replace human relationships. Thus, a deterioration of these human relations can potentially destroy the organization.

Envy and other relationship diseases develop in the workplace when the "other" becomes an "object-other" and/or a "competing other". In envy, the other is considered as an object reflected in a mirror, rather than as a human being who has desires, complexities, qualities, and limitations. When organizations reduce human beings to quantifiable objects that can be measured, evaluated, and compared, or to figures that are supposed to represent their performance – this is, when they evaluate individuals without taking into account the qualities that make them autonomous subjects – envy is bound to develop. A healthy relationship is based on the recognition of the other as a subject. When people are reduced to objects, the bonds that should link them to others cannot develop and their sense of belonging to the group cannot exist.

"Killing the brother" in the workplace

The other is also often reduced to a "competing other", an obsessing, threatening double who must be fought. Competition is a fundamental aspect of life in western societies. However, it took an invisible turn for the worst with the implementation of management systems that use direct competition *between* people as a driving force behind organizations.

Competition between two or more organizations generally implies cooperation between the members of the same organization; this enables individuals to experience the "other" no longer as a rival or a "competing other" but as the "other of collaboration". The fact that the competition takes place between organizations rather than between individuals serves as a protecting shield for the person. It enables the individual to sublimate his/her desire to confront the other in a framework that gives structure to the competition and that serves as a mediator between them.[3] The confrontation is not direct; it does not take place between individuals but between different, clearly identified organizations with their own, different histories that have competed against one another for a long time.

What is tragic about contemporary organizations is the fact that competition is no longer only external, but also internal. External competition has not stopped but it is used more and more to justify the fact that the main competition actually takes place internally, within the organization between individuals who confront one another directly. Competition becomes an inter-personal confrontation in which the subject finds it difficult to experience the other as "the collaborating other". Individuals are subjected to intense and permanent rivalry, and rivalry becomes the only thing that bonds people. It is not the "father" that the subject needs to kill but the "brother" – an act condemned in all societies. Isn't this where the transgression lies? In openly driving the subject to annihilate an "other" whom he/she perceives, fantasmatically, as an obstacle?

No one can escape the question of how one relates to others, because nobody lives in total isolation. This question is fundamental in organizations; it points to the relations we develop with the person we have to work with. Thus, we are confronted with the inescapable difficulty of having to work with others. On the one hand, there is the risk of merging with the other and losing one's own identity. On the other, there is the risk of reducing the other to a mere object that one will compare oneself with, or even want to eliminate!

In between these extreme scenarios, there is one that we can help create through our everyday actions: a scenario where the other is respected as a subject instead of being exploited as an object; one who is accepted with all his/her differences, and whose characteristics are perceived as assets. To overcome envy, we must be able to perceive and accept the other as a person we are bound to by the bonds of humanity. To transcend envy, we must ask ourselves what we can share with the other, rather than what we can take from him.

Notes

Introduction

1. Data collected by the author.
2. The description of this case is based on Stein (2000a).
3. Case drawn from Halton (1994).
4. Kets de Vries (1992; 1995).
5. Babiak (1995); Berdahl (2007); Dejours (1980); Frost (2003); Raver and Gelfand (2005); Hirigoyen (1998); Zapf and Leymann (1996).

Chapter 1

1. Quoted from Behm (2002).
2. Vidaillet (2008).
3. Kant (1785; 1983).
4. Schimmel (2008).
5. Rousseau J.-J. (1762; 1966).
6. Parrott (1991); Salovey and Rodin (1989); Parrott and Smith (1993).
7. Klein (1957). Psychoanalyst of the English school of psychoanalysis, she was the first to have studied envy, in the 1950s.
8. Parrott (1991).
9. Ibid.
10. This was demonstrated by Melanie Klein (1957) (see Vidaillet, 2008). Many social psychologists have acknowledged the potentially unconscious dimension of envy (for instance, Alicke, 2008; or Smith and Kim, 2007).
11. Silver and Sabini (1978a).
12. Silver and Sabini (1978b).
13. Schoeck (1969, p. 15 in the French edition).
14. Alberoni (1995); Hassoun-Lestienne (1998a); Leach (2008); Parrott (1991); Schoeck (1969); Smith and Combs (2008); Smith and Kim (2007).
15. Alicke (2008).
16. This is at the basis of social psychology: Festinger (1954); Tesser and Campbell (1980).
17. Smith, Parrott and Diener (1990).
18. Spinoza (1677; 2005, vol. III).
19. DePaola (2001); Parrott and Smith (1993).
20. Silver and Sabini (1978b).
21. Salovey and Rodin (1984).
22. Parrott (1991).
23. Parrott and Smith (1993).
24. Ibid.

25. Klein (1957); Smith (1991); Smith and Kim (2007); Vidaillet (2008).
26. Smith and Combs (2008).
27. Hassoun-Lestienne (1998a); Schoeck (1969).
28. Polizzi (2005).
29. Alberoni (1995); Hassoun-Lestienne (1998b); Klein (1957); Smith and Kim (2007); Smith and Combs (2008); Vidaillet (2008).
30. Vidaillet (2008).
31. Baudelaire, "Une mort héroïque", in *Le Spleen de Paris*.
32. This was discussed mostly by Melanie Klein and her followers in the English school of psychoanalysis.
33. See Parrott (1991, pp. 13–15); Smith and Kim (2007); Smith and Combs (2008); Alberoni (1995); Klein (1957); Vidaillet (2007; 2008).
34. Parrott and Smith (1993).
35. La Rochefoucauld, maxime 28.

Chapter 2

1. Salovey and Rodin (1984).
2. Schaubroeck and Lam (2004).
3. Weick (1995).
4. Boudens (2005, p. 1303).
5. Weick and Roberts (1993, p. 374).
6. Duffy and Shaw (2000).
7. Schlapobersky (1994); Halton (1994); Stein (2000a, 2000b).
8. Vecchio (2005).
9. Vecchio (1995).
10. Vecchio (2000).
11. Graen and Uhl-Bien (1995).
12. Sullivan (1956, p. 133) quoted in Smith and Combs (2008).
13. Klein (1957); Smith (1991); Smith et al. (1994); Smith and Kim (2007); Smith and Combs (2008).
14. Alberoni (1995).
15. Vidaillet (2007).
16. Salovey and Rodin (1984); Smith et al. (1994, 1999).
17. Klein (1957).
18. Vecchio (1995).
19. Mouly and Sankaran (2002).
20. Leader (1996).
21. Pushkin (1965).
22. Klein (1957); Parks et al. (2002).
23. Zizzo (2008).
24. Stein (2005).
25. Exline and Lobel (1999).
26. Mouly and Sankaran (2002).
27. Vecchio (1995).
28. Vecchio (1995, 2000).

29. Alberoni (1995); Patient *et al.* (2003); Sabini and Silver (1986); Schoeck (1969).
30. Plutchik (2002); Smith and Kim (2007).
31. Foster (1972, p. 166).
32. Patient *et al.* (2003).
33. Kets de Vries (1992).
34. Vecchio (1995, p. 206).
35. Stein (1997).
36. Epstein (2003); Lapham (1989).
37. Schaubroeck and Lam (2004).
38. Parrott (1991); Vidaillet (2008).
39. Patient *et al.* (2003).
40. Leach (2008); Smith (1991); Smith *et al.* (1994); Schoeck (1969).
41. Adams (1965); Cropanzano (1993); Folger and Cropanzano (1998); Greenberg and Colquitt (2005).
42. Schoeck (1969), pp. 323–324 in the French edition (Schoeck, 1995).
43. Freud also discusses this issue in Chapter 9 of his essay *Group Psychology and The Analysis of the Ego* (1921). According to him, the demand for social justice and equality is a direct consequence of envy: "Social justice means that we deny ourselves many things so that others may have to do without them too, or cannot demand them for themselves, which is the same" (Freud, 1921, p. 147 of French version).
44. Rawls (1971). See also Smith (1991).
45. Smith (1991); Smith *et al.* (1994).

Chapter 3

1. Maslow (1954).
2. Herzberg (1966).
3. Alderfer (1972).
4. Vroom (1964).
5. Adams (1965).
6. Ibid., p. 280.
7. Dupuy (1979).
8. Jenkins (2005).
9. Dupuy (1979).
10. Belk (2008).
11. Girard (1965, p. 19 in French edition, our translation).
12. Girard (1965).
13. Dumouchel (1979, p. 168, our translation).
14. Schaubroeck and Lam (2004).

Chapter 4

1. I refer here to societies founded on socialist and collectivist ideals. However, according to John Rawls, for example, true equalitarian societies are to be found in the Western democracies that give their

citizens equal rights but which do not as a result cause a homogenization of the population.
2. Schoeck (1969, Chapter 17), who uses the anthropological research on kibbutzim (1930–1960) and in particular that conducted by Spiro (1958).
3. Stein (2000b).
4. Data collected by the author.
5. Vidaillet (2006)
6. Interview with the director.
7. Enjeux-Les Échos (Octobre 2005).
8. Broadbridge (2002).
9. Weber (2005).
10. Ritzer (1996).
11. Brunsson *et al.* (2000) show to what extent the development of standardization has become crucial in the management of not only organizations, but also developed societies in general.
12. Official web site: www.iso.ch/iso/fr/aboutiso/introduction/index.html
13. Townley *et al.* (2003).
14. Slovic and Mac Phillamy (1974).
15. Weber (2005).
16. Ritzer (1996).
17. Pfeffer and Fong (2004).
18. www.iso.ch/iso/fr/aboutiso/introduction/index.html
19. Hammer and Champy (1994).
20. Hassoun-Lestienne (1998a, p. 19); Vidaillet (2008).
21. Schoeck (1969); Girard (1977); Foster (1972); Salovey and Rothman (1991).
22. Data collected by the author.
23. Pfeffer (1998); Pfeffer and Sutton (2006).
24. Novations Group.
25. Pfeffer and Langton (1993).
26. Cowherd and Levine (1992).
27. Bloom and Michel (2002).
28. Bloom (1999).
29. Foster (1972); Dupuy (1979).
30. Bedeian (1995).
31. Beauvois and Dubois (1988); Morris and Peng (1994).
32. Vecchio (1995).
33. Berry (1983).
34. Vecchio (2005).
35. Data collected by the author.

Chapter 5

1. See Lacan's theory of the Mirror phase (1966a).
2. Lacan (1966b).
3. Lacan (1966c; 1978; 2004).
4. I place myself, here, in a Lacanian perspective. Lacan proposed a new extended interpretation of Freud's Oedipus complex theory.

5. It is what psychoanalysts call "castration".
6. Lacan (1957–1958).
7. Hassoun-Lestienne (1998b).
8. Vidaillet (2007, 2008).
9. Lacan (1986).
10. Pagès *et al.* (1979); Aubert and de Gaulejac (1991); Enriquez (1997); Aubert (2004); Weber (2005).
11. Aubert and de Gaulejac (1991, p. 111; our translation).
12. Ibid., p. 268; our translation.
13. Aubert and de Gaulejac (1991); Enriquez (1997); Rhéaume (2004).
14. Aubert and de Gaulejac (1991, p. 123).
15. De Gaulejac (2004).
16. These are V. de Gaulejac's expressions (2004; our translation).
17. Diary, February 9th, 1999.
18. March 27th, 2002.
19. Richard Durn's diary, January 2nd, 2002.
20. My interpretation of Richard Durn's case.
21. De Gaulejac (2004, p. 141).
22. Aubert and de Gaulejac (1991, p. 184–190). I take full responsibility for the interpretation I propose here of the data presented by these authors. The introduction of the concept of envy in this interpretation is also of my own doing.
23. Aubert and de Gaulejac (1991, p. 188).
24. Ibid., p. 189.
25. Ibid., p. 186.
26. Ibid., p. 187.
27. Ibid., p. 204.
28. Heyberger (2005).
29. Ibid., p. 73; our translation.
30. Ibid., p. 76; our translation.
31. Ibid., p. 74; our translation.

Chapter 6

1. Ashkanazy *et al.* (2000); Payne and Cooper (2001); Boudens (2005).
2. Maitlis and Ozcelik (2004).
3. Terrion and Ashforth (2002).
4. Frost (2003).
5. Ibid.
6. Ibid.
7. Kotter and Cohen (2002).
8. Kiefer (2005).
9. Data collected by the author.
10. Data collected by the author.
11. Kets de Vries (1993).
12. Kets de Vries and Miller (1984).

13. Baum (1992, p. 324).
14. Schimmel (2008).
15. Ibid.
16. Sias *et al.* (2004).
17. Shaubroeck and Lam (2004).
18. Duffy *et al.* (2008).
19. Poulson *et al.* (2005); Stein (2005); Vecchio (1995).
20. Poulson *et al.* (2005).
21. Smith (1991).
22. Bourdieu (1984); Ferris and King (1991); Bozionelos (2005).
23. Vidaillet (2008).
24. Klein (1957); Smith (1991); Smith and Kim (2007); Smith and Combs (2008); Vidaillet (2008).
25. Klein (1957); see also Vidaillet (2008).
26. Stern (2004).
27. Vidaillet (2002).
28. Stein (1997).
29. See Vidaillet (2008).

Chapter 7

1. Vecchio (1995).
2. Stein (2005).
3. Prigent (2003).
4. Vecchio (1995).
5. Data collected by the author.
6. Exline and Zell (2008).
7. Exline and Zell (2008).
8. Schoeck (1995, p. 14).
9. In psychoanalysis, it refers to the process of obtaining additional insight into personality changes in a patient through repeated and varied examination of a conflict or problem. Free association, analysis of a patient's resistances and transference, and interpretation constitute the fundamental facets of this process.
10. Adapted from Bedeian (1995) and Exline and Zell (2008).

Conclusion

1. Dupuy (1979); Dumouchel (1979).
2. Wilhelm (2005, p. 10–11).
3. Palazzi (2006) provides a helpful description of the differences between competition at market level – which can enable a person to sublimate his/her desire to attack the other – and competition in the organization – which prevents him/her from positioning himself/herself as a subject and which takes place at the expense of his/her mental health.

References

Core references

Foster, G. M., "The anatomy of envy: a study in symbolic behaviour", *Current Anthropology*, 13(2), 165–202, 1972.

Girard, R., *Deceit, Desire and the Novel: Self and Other in Literary Structure*, Baltimore: Johns Hopkins University Press, 1965 (first published in 1961 as *Mensonge romantique et verité romanesque*).

Hassoun-Lestienne, P. (ed.), *L'envie et le désir. Les faux-frères*, coll. Morales, no. 24, Autrement, 13–58, 1998a.

Klein, M., *Envy and Gratitude*, London: Tavistock Publications, 1957.

Salovey, P. (ed.), *The Psychology of Envy and Jealousy*, New York: The Guilford Press, 271–286. 1991.

Schoeck, H., *Envy: A Theory of Social Behavior*, New York: Harcourt, Brace, and World, 1969 (first German edition: *der Neid*, 1966).

Smith, R. H. (ed.), *The Psychology of Envy*, New York: Oxford University Press, 2008.

Stein, M., "After Eden: envy and the defences against anxiety paradigm", *Human Relations*, 53(2), 193–212, 2000b.

Vecchio, R. P., "It's not easy being green: jealousy and envy in the workplace", in K. R. Rowland, and G. R. Ferris (eds), *Research in Personal and Human Resource Management*, JAI Press, 13, 201–244, 1995.

Vidaillet, B., "A Lacanian theory's contribution to the study of workplace envy: a case study", *Human Relations*, 60(11), 1669–1700, 2007.

Other references cited in the book

Adams, J. S., "Inequity in social exchanges", in L. Berkowitz (ed.), *Advances in Experimental Social Psychology*, vol. 2, New York Academic Press, 267–300, 1965.

Alberoni, F., *Les envieux*, Paris: Plon, 1995.

Alderfer, C. P., *Existence, Relatedness, and Growth: Human Needs in Organizational Settings*, New York: Free Press, 1972.

Alicke, M. D., "Self-comparison and envy", in R. H. Smith (ed.), *The Psychology of Envy*, Oxford University Press, 2008.

Ashkanazy, N. M., Hartel, C. E, and Zerbe, W. J., *Emotions in the Workplace: Research, Theory and Practice*, Quorum Books, 2000.

Aubert, N., "Un individu paradoxal", in N. Aubert (ed.), *L'individu hypermoderne*, Paris: Erès, 12–24, 2004.

Aubert, N. and de Gaulejac, V., *Le coût de l'excellence*, Paris: Seuil, 1991.

Babiak, P., "When psychopaths go to work: a case study of an industrial psychopath", *Applied Psychology: An International Review*, 44(2), 171–188, 1995.

Baudelaire, C., *Le Spleen de Paris: petits poèmes en prose,* Paris: Poche, 1869, 2003.

Baum, H. S., "Mentoring: narcissistic fantasies and oedipal realities", *Human Relations,* 45(3): 223–245, 1992.

Beauvois, J. -L. and Dubois, N., "The norm of internality in the explanation of psychological events", *European Journal of Social Psychology,* 18, 299–316, 1988.

Bedeian, A. G., "Workplace envy", *Organizational Dynamics,* 23(4), 49–56, 1995.

Behm, C. A., *L'envie et la déformation du désir,* www.enneagramme.com/Articles/2002/EM_0205_a2.htm, 2002.

Belk, R. W., "Envy and marketing", in R. H. Smith (ed.), *The Psychology of Envy,* New York: Oxford University Press, 2008.

Berdahl, J. L., "Harassment based on sex: protecting social status in the context of gender hierarchy", *Academy of Management Review,* 32(2), 641–658, 2007.

Berry, M., *Une technologie invisible – Impact des outils de gestion sur les systèmes sociaux complexes,* Paris: Publication Ecole Polytechnique, 1983.

Bloom, M., "The performance effects of pay dispersion on individuals and organizations", *Academy of Management Journal,* 42(1), 25–40, 1999.

Bloom, M. and Michel, J. G., "The relationships among organizational context, pay, dispersion, and among managerial turnover", *Academy of Management Journal,* 45(1), 33–42, 2002.

Boudens, C. J., "The story of work: a narrative analysis of workplace emotion", *Organization Studies,* 26(9), 1285–1306, 2005.

Bourdieu, P., *Homo academicus,* Paris: Editions de Minuit, 1984.

Bozionelos, N., "When the inferior candidate is offered the job: the selection interview as a political and power game", *Human Relations,* 58(12), 1605–1631, 2005.

Broadbridge, A., "Retail managers: their work stressors and coping strategies", *Journal of Retailing and Consumer Services,* 9(3), 173–183, 2002.

Brunsson, N. and Jacobsson, B. (eds), *A World of Standards,* Oxford University Press, 2000.

Cowherd, D. M. and Levine, D. I., "Product quality and pay equity between lower- level employees and top management: an investigation of distributive justice theory", *Administrative Science Quarterly,* 37, 302–320, 1992.

Cropanzano, R. (ed.), *Justice in the Workplace: Approaching Fairness in Human Resource Management,* Hillsdale, NJ: Lawrence Erlbaum, 1993.

De Gaulejac, V., "Le sujet manqué. L'individu face aux contradictions de l'hyper- modernité", in N. Aubert (ed.), *L'individu hypermoderne,* Erès, 129–143, 2004.

Dejours, C., *Le travail, usure mentale: essai de psychopathologie du travail,* Paris: Editions du Centurion, 1980.

DePaola, H., "Envy, jealousy and shame", *International Journal of Psychoanalysis,* 82, 381–384, 2001.

Duffy, M. K. and Shaw, J. D., "The Salieri syndrome: consequences of envy in groups", *Small Group Research,* 31, 3–23, 2000.

Duffy, M. K., Shaw, J. D., and Schaubroeck J. M., "Envy in organizational life", in R. H. Smith (ed.), *The Psychology of Envy,* Oxford University Press, 2008.

Dumouchel, P., "L'ambivalence de la rareté", in P. Dumouchel and J. -P. Dupuy (eds), *L'enfer des choses, René Girard et la logique de l'économie,* Paris: Seuil, 1979.

Dupuy, J. P., "Le signe et l'envie", in P. Dumouchel, J. -P. Dupuy (eds), *L'enfer des choses, René Girard et la logique de l'économie,* Paris: Seuil, 1979.

Enjeux-Les Échos, n° 217, octobre 2005.

Enriquez, E., *Les jeux du pouvoir et du désir dans l'entreprise,* Paris: Desclée de Brouwer, 1997.

Epstein, J., *Envy,* Oxford University Press, 2003.

Exline, J. J. and Lobel, M., "The perils of outperformance: sensitivity about being the target of a threatening upward comparison", *Psychological Bulletin,* 125, 307–337, 1999.

Exline, J. J. and Zell, A. L., "Antidotes to envy: a conceptual framework", in R. H. Smith (ed.), *The Psychology of Envy,* New York: Oxford University Press, 2008.

Ferris, G. R. and King, T. R., "Politics in human resources decisions: a walk on the dark side", *Organizational Dynamics,* 20(2), 59–71, 1991.

Festinger, L., "A theory of social comparison processes", *Human Relations,* 7, 117–140, 1954.

Folger, R. and Cropanzano, R., *Organizational Justice and Human Resource Management,* Thousand Oaks, CA: Sage, 1998.

Freud, S., *Group Psychology and the Analysis of the Ego. The Standard Edition,* vol. 18, London: Hogarth Press, 67–143, 1921.

Frost, P., *Toxic Emotions at Work,* Harvard Business School Press, 2003.

Girard, R., *Violence and the Sacred,* Baltimore: Johns Hopkins University Press, 1977 (first published in 1972 as *La violence et le sacré*).

Girard, R., *To Double Business Bound: Essays on Literature, Mimesis and Anthropology,* Baltimore: Johns Hopkins University Press, 1978.

Girard, R., *The Scapegoat,* Baltimore: Johns Hopkins University Press, 1986 (first published in 1982 as *Le bouc émissaire*).

Girard, R., *Job: The Victim of his People,* Stanford: Stanford University Press, 1987 (first published in 1985 as *La route antique des hommes pervers*).

Girard, R., *A Theater of Envy: William Shakespeare,* Oxford University Press, 1991 (first published in 1990 as *Shakespeare: les feux de l'envie*).

Graen, G. and Uhl-Bien, M., "Relationship-based approach to leadership: development of leader-member exchange (LMX) theory of leadership over 25 years", *Leadership Quarterly,* 2, 219–247, 1995.

Greenberg, J. and Colquitt, J. A. (eds), *Handbook of Organizational Justice,* Mahah, NJ: Lawrence Erlbaum Associates, 2005.

Halton, W., "Some unconscious aspects of organizational life: contributions from psychoanalysis", in A. Obholzer and V. Z. Roberts (eds), *The Unconscious at Work: Individual and Organizational Stress in the Human Services,* London: Routledge, 11–18, 1994.

Hammer, M. and Champy, J., *Reengineering the Corporation: A Manifesto for Business Revolution,* New York: Harper Business, 1994.

Hassoun-Lestienne, P., "Malade d'envie", in P. Hassoun-Lestienne (ed.), *L'envie et le désir. Les faux-frères,* coll. Morales, no. 24, Autrement, 13–58, 1998b.

Herzberg, F., *Work and the Nature of Man,* New York: The Mentor Executive Library, 1966.

Heyberger, B., "L'envie au couvent", in F. Wilhelm (ed.), *L'Envie et ses figurations littéraires,* Editions universitaires de Dijon, 71–83, Dijon: 2005.

Hirigoyen, M. F., *Le harcèlement moral, la violence perverse au quotidien,* Paris: Syros, 1998.

Jenkins, P., "Entretien", in *Paul Jenkins – Œuvres majeures,* catalogue de l'exposition, musée des Beaux-Arts de Lille, 2005.

Kant, E., *Fondements de la métaphysique des mœurs,* 1785, Paris: Livre de Poche, 1993.

Kets de Vries, M. F., "The motivating role of envy: a forgotten factor in management theory", *Administration & Society,* 24, 41–60, 1992.

Kets de Vries, M. F., *Leaders, Fools, and Impostors,* San Francisco: Jossey-Bass, 1993.

Kets de Vries, M. F., *Life and Death in the Executive Fast Lane: Essays on Irrational Organizations and Their Leaders,* San Francisco: Jossey-Bass, 1995.

Kets de Vries, M. F. and Miller D., *The Neurotic Organization: Diagnosing and Changing Counterproductive Styles of Management,* San Francisco: Jossey-Bass, 1984.

Kiefer, T., "Feeling bad: antecedents and consequences of negative emotions in ongoing change", *Journal of Organizational Behavior,* 26(8), 875–897, 2005.

Kotter, J. P., *A Force for Change: How Leadership Differs from Management,* New York: Free Press, 1990.

Kotter, J. P. and Cohen, D. S., *The Heart of Change,* Harvard Business School Press, 2002.

La Rochefoucauld, F., *Maximes,* Paris: Garnier Flammarion, 1977.

Lacan, J., *Les formations de l'inconscient,* Séminaire inédit, 1957–1958.

Lacan, J., "Le stade du miroir comme formateur de la fonction du 'Je' telle qu'elle nous est révélée dans l'expérience psychanalytique", in *Écrits,* Paris: Seuil, 1966a.

Lacan, J., "De nos antecedents", in *Écrits,* Paris: Seuil, 1966b.

Lacan, J., "Introduction au commentaire de Jean Hyppolite sur la *Verneigung* de Freud", in *Écrits,* Paris: Seuil, 1966c.

Lacan, J., *Le Séminaire – Le Moi dans la théorie de Freud et dans la technique de la psychanalyse,* livre 2, 1954–1955, coll. Champ freudien, Paris: Seuil, 1978.

Lacan, J., *Le Séminaire – L'éthique de la psychanalyse,* livre 7, 1959–1960. Paris: Seuil, 1986.

Lacan, J., *Le Séminaire – L'angoisse,* livre 10, 1962–1963, Paris: Seuil, 2004.

Lapham, L. H., *Money and Class in America: Notes and Observations on the Civil Religion,* New York: Ballantine, 1989.

Leach, C. W., "Envy, inferiority, and injustice: three bases of anger about inequality", in R. H. Smith (ed.), *The Psychology of Envy,* New York: Oxford University Press, 2008.

Leader, D., *Why do Women Write More Letters than they Post?,* London: Faber and Faber, 1996.

Maitlis, S. and Ozcelik, H., "Toxic decision processes: a study of emotion and organizational decision making", *Organization Science,* 15(4), 375–393, 2004.

Maslow, A., *Motivation and Personality,* New York: Harper, 1954.

Morris, M. W. and Peng, K. P., "Culture and cause: American and Chinese attributions for social and physical events", *Journal of Personality and Social Psychology,* 67, 949–971, 1994.

Mouly, V. S. and Sankaran, J. K., "The enactment of envy within organizations", *Journal of Applied Behavioral Science,* 38(1), 36–57, 2002.

Pagès, M., Bonetti, M., de Gaulejac, V., and Descendre, D., *L'emprise de l'organisation,* Paris: PUF, 1979.

Palazzi, S., "Beyond competition: excellence, psychic stakes and clinical effects", *Symposium of the International Society for the Psychoanalytical Study of Organisations,* 2006.

Parks, C. D., Rumble, A. C., and Posey, D. C., "The effects of envy on reciprocation in a social dilemma", *Personality and Social Psychology Bulletin,* 28, 509–520, 2002.

Parrott, W. G., "The emotional experiences of envy and jealousy", in P. Salovey (ed.), *The Psychology of Envy and Jealousy,* The Guilford Press, 3–30, 1991.

Parrott, W. G. and Smith, R. H., "Distinguishing the experiences of envy and jealousy", *Journal of Personality and Social Psychology,* 64(6), 906–920, 1993.

Patient, D., Lawrence, T. B., and Maitlis, S., "Understanding workplace envy through narrative fiction", *Organization Studies,* 24(7), 1015–1044, 2003.

Payne, R. L. and Cooper, C. L. (eds), *Emotions at Work: Theory, Research and Applications in Management,* Chichester: John Wiley and Sons, 2001.

Pfeffer, J., "The human equation: building profits by putting people first", Harvard Business School Press, 1998.

Pfeffer, J. and Fong, C. T., "The business school 'business': some lessons from the U.S. experience", *Journal of Management Studies,* 41, 1501–1520, 2004.

Pfeffer, J. and Langton, N., "The effect of wage dispersion on satisfaction, productivity, and working collaboratively: evidence from college ad university faculty", *Administrative Science Quarterly,* 38(3), 382–407, 1993.

Pfeffer, J. and Sutton, R. I., "Evidence-based management", *Harvard Business Review,* 84(1), 63–74, 2006.

Plutchik, R., *Emotions and Life: Perspectives from Psychology, Biology, and Evolution,* Washington, D.C.: American Psychological Association, 2002.

Polizzi, G., "L''enfant désallaité'", in F. Wilhelm (ed.), *L'Envie et ses figurations littéraires,* Editions universitaires de Dijon, 119–143, Dijon: 2005.

Poulson, C., Duncan, J., and Massie, M., "'I am not what I am': destructive emotions in an organizational hierarchy: the case of Othello and Iago", in N. M. Ashkanazy (ed.), *The Effect of Affect in Organizational Settings. Research on Emotion in Organizations,* London: Elsevier Science, 1, 211–240, 2005.

Prigent, Y., *La cruauté ordinaire. Où est le Mal?,* Paris: Desclée de Brouwer, 2003.

Pushkin, A., *Little Tragedies* (Translated by E. M. Kayden; original work published in 1830), Yellow Springs: The Antioch Press, 1965.

Raver, J. and Gelfand, M., "Beyond the individual victim: linking sexual harassment, team processes, and team performance", *Academy of Management Journal,* 48(3), 387–400, 2005.

Rawls, J., *A Theory of Justice,* Cambridge, MA: Harvard University Press, 1971.

Rhéaume, J., "L'hyperactivité au travail: entre narcissisme et identité", in N. Aubert (ed.), *L'individu hypermoderne*, Erès, 89–102, 2004.

Ritzer, G., *The McDonaldization of Society*, New York: Sage, 1996.

Rousseau, J. J., *Émile ou de l'éducation*, 1762, Paris: Flammarion, 1966.

Sabini, J. and Silver, M., "Envy", in R. Harré (ed.)., *The social construction of emotions*, Oxford: Basil Blackwell, 167–183, 1986.

Salovey, P. and Rodin, J., "Some antecedents and consequences of social comparison jealousy", *Journal of Personality and Social Psychology*, 47, 780–792, 1984.

Salovey, P. and Rodin, J., "Envy and jealousy in close relationships", in C. Hendrick (ed.), *Review of Personality and Social Psychology*, vol. 10, Close relationships, Newbury Park, CA: Sage, 221–246, 1989.

Salovey, P. and Rothman, A. J., "Envy and jealousy: self and society", in P. Salovey (ed.), *The Psychology of Envy and Jealousy*, The Guilford Press, 271–286, 1991.

Schaubroeck, J. and Lam, S. S. K., "Comparing lots before and after: promotion rejectees' invidious reactions to promotees", *Organizational Behavior and Human Decision Processes*, 94, 33–47, 2004.

Schimmel, S., "Envy in Jewish thought and literature", in R. H. Smith (ed.), *The Psychology of Envy*, New York: Oxford University Press, 2008.

Schlapobersky, J., "The language of the group: Monologue, dialogue and discourse in group analysis", in D. Brown and L. Zinkin (eds), *The Psyche and the Social World: Developments in Group-Analytic Theory*, London: Routledge, 211–231, 1994.

Schoeck, H., *L'envie. Une histoire du mal*, Paris: Les Belles Lettres, 1995.

Sias, P. M., Heath, R. G., Perry, T., Silva, D., and Fix, B., "Narratives of workplace friendship deterioration", *Journal of Social and Personal Relationships*, 21(3), 321–340, 2004.

Silver, M. and Sabini, J., "The social construction of envy", *Journal for the Theory of Social Behavior*, 8, 313–332, 1978a.

Silver, M. and Sabini, J., "The perception of envy", *Social Psychology Quarterly*, 41, 105–117, 1978b.

Slovic, P. and Mac Phillamy, D. J., "Dimensional commensurability and cue utilization", *Comparative Judgment, Organizational Behavior and Human Performance*, 11, 172–194, 1974.

Smith, R. H., "Envy and the sense of injustice", in P. Salovey (ed.), *The Psychology of Envy and Jealousy*, The Guilford Press, 79–99, 1991.

Smith, R. H. and Combs, D. J. Y., "Never at heart's ease: envy and the challenges to good health", in R. H. Smith (ed.), *The Psychology of Envy*, New York: Oxford University Press, 2008.

Smith, R. H. and Kim, S. H., "Comprehending envy", *Psychological Bulletin*, 133(1), 46–64, 2007.

Smith, R. H., Parrott, W. G., and Diener, E., *The Development of a Scale for Measuring Enviousness*, Unpublished manuscript, 1990.

Smith, R. H., Parrott, W. G., Ozer, D., and Moniz, A., "Subjective injustice and inferiority as predictors of hostile and depressive feelings in envy", *Journal of Personality and Social Psychology*, 20, 717–723, 1994.

Smith, R. H., Parrott, W. G., Diener, E. F., Hoyle, R. H., and Kim, S., "Dispositional envy", *Personality and Social Psychology Bulletin*, 25, 1007–1020, 1999.

Spinoza, B., *Ethics*, 1677, London: Penguin Classics, 2005.

Spiro, M., *Children of the Kibbutz*, Cambridge University Press, 1958.

Stein, M., "Envy and leadership", *European Journal of Work and Organizational Psychology*, 6(4), 435–465, 1997.

Stein, M., "'Winners' training and its trouble", *Personnel Review*, 29(4), 445–460, 2000a.

Stein, M., "The Othello conundrum: the inner contagion of leadership", *Organization Studies*, 26(9), 1405–1419, 2005.

Stern, A. -L., *Le savoir déporté. Camps, histoire, psychanalyse*, Paris: Seuil, 2004.

Sullivan, H. S., *Clinical Studies in Psychiatry*, New York: W. W. Norton, 1956.

Terrion, J. L. and Ashforth, B. E., "From 'I' to 'We': the role of putdown humor in the development of a temporary group", *Human Relations*, 55(1), 55–88, 2002.

Tesser, A. and Campbell, J., "Self-definition: the impact of the relative performance and similarity of others", *Social Psychology Quarterly*, 43, 341–347, 1980.

Townley, B., Cooper, D. J., and Oakes, L., "Performance measures and the rationalization of organizations", *Organization Studies*, 24(7), 1045–1071, 2003.

Vecchio, R. P., "Negative emotion in the workplace: employee jealousy and envy", *International Journal of Stress Management*, 7, 161–179, 2000.

Vecchio, R. P., "Explorations in employee envy: feeling envious and feeling envied", *Cognition and Emotion*, 19(1), 69–81, 2005.

Vidaillet, B., *Le cas Tracta: perception, conflit et décision en entreprise*, Paris: Centrale des Cas et des Médias Pédagogiques, 2002.

Vidaillet, B., "Competition, rivalry and envy at the workplace: a Lacanian perspective", *Symposium of the International Society for the Psychoanalytical Study of Organisations*, Amsterdam, 2006.

Vidaillet, B., "A Lacanian theory's contribution to the study of workplace envy: a case study", *Human Relations*, 60(11), 1669–1700, 2007.

Vidaillet, B., "Psychoanalytic contributions to understanding envy: classic and contemporary perspectives", in R. H. Smith (ed.), *The Psychology of Envy*, New York: Oxford University Press, 2008.

Vroom, V., *Work and Motivation*, New York: John Wiley and Sons, 1964.

Weber, H., *Du ketchup dans les veines – Pourquoi les employés adhèrent-ils à l'organisation chez McDonald's?*, coll. Sociologie clinique, Paris: Erès, 2005.

Weick, K., *Sensemaking in Organizations*, Newbury Park, CA: Sage, 1995.

Weick, K. and Roberts, K., "Collective mind in organizations: heedful interrelating on flight decks, *Administrative Science Quarterly*, 38, 357–381, 1993.

Wilhelm, F., "La tristesse du bien d'autrui: une passion *oubliée* par la critique", in F. Wilhelm (ed.), *L'Envie et ses figurations littéraires*, Editions universitaires de Dijon, 5–18, Dijon: 2005.

Zapf, D. and Leymann, H. (eds), "Mobbing and Victimization at Work", *A Special Issue of The European Journal of Work and Organizational Psychology*, 2, 1996.

Zizzo, D. J., "The Cognitive and Behavioral Economics of Envy", in R. H. Smith, (ed.), *The Psychology of Envy*, New York: Oxford University Press, 2008.

Index